MAGIC
for
CHANGE

MAGIC
for
CHANGE

spells and rituals for social transformation

CERRIDWEN GREENLEAF

CICO BOOKS
LONDON NEW YORK

Published in 2023 by CICO Books
An imprint of Ryland Peters & Small Ltd
20–21 Jockey's Fields   341 E 116th St
London WC1R 4BW   New York, NY 10029

www.rylandpeters.com

10 9 8 7 6 5 4 3 2 1

A CIP catalog record for this book is available from the
Library of Congress and the British Library.

ISBN: 978-1-80065-262-0

Printed in China

Illustrator: Barbara Tamilin
For other picture credits, see page 144

Commissioning editor: Kristine Pidkameny
Editor: Kristy Richardson
Senior designer: Emily Breen
Art director: Sally Powell
Creative director: Leslie Harrington
Production manager: Gordana Simakovic
Publishing manager: Penny Craig

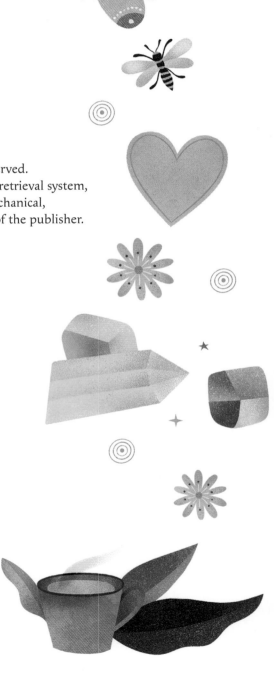

Contents

INTRODUCTION 6

Warrior Witches and Covens

CHAPTER 1

ALTAR-ATIONS 8

Creating a Home Altar
for Positive Change

CHAPTER 2

**SAVING MOTHER
EARTH 24**

Facing Climate Change
to Protect the Source of All Life

CHAPTER 3

**PEACE, LOVE,
AND HEALING 42**

Rituals to End Conflict,
Gun Violence, and War

CHAPTER 4

MAY ALL BE FED 56

Conjuring Abundance to
Help End Hunger

CHAPTER 5

**FEMINIST
WITCHCRAFT 70**

Enchantments for Equality
and Power Potions

CHAPTER 6

**MANIFESTING
MAGIC 96**

Prosperity Spells and Money
Charms for the Greater Good

CHAPTER 7

**RITUALS FOR
RECLAIMING 114**

Witches as Activists
for Social Justice

CHAPTER 8

**CO-CREATING
BLESSINGS 128**

Rituals for Groups
and Solo Spellcasters

Resources 141 • Index 142 • Acknowledgments 144

INTRODUCTION

Warrior Witches and Covens

Witchcraft is communal by nature. Pagans have a deep connection to the Earth, and maintain a close community with friends, family, and neighbors—essentially, their tribe. At the very core of their craft is the coven—a group of practitioners working together for the good of their tribe or community.

In earlier times, high holidays and seasonal celebrations were all about community, making sure there was prosperity and good health, and ensuring good weather and plentiful crops so there would be enough food for everyone. This has been a part of witchcraft from the beginning and, I daresay, is more important now than ever before. Today, witches continually advocate for positive change with every spell and ritual—they set magical intentions to create better outcomes in their own lives, as well as those of their loved ones, their community—and the world.

While it may not always be obvious, witches are optimists. Setting intentions and magical workings are acts of positivity—the belief that the future can be made better with the tools and rituals of the craft. From solo spells and calming crystals through protection magic, energy-raising enchantments, and money manifestation, these are the tools needed to quell contention, support peaceful protest, replace conflict with

loving compatibility, and even help those fleeing war zones or natural disaster. To stem the tide of global warning, improve the land, and encourage less planet-harming meat consumption and more plant-based living, there are plenty of planet-positive rites featured in this guide, including tree-planting charms, guerilla gardening, and green witchery, which are good for both Mother Earth and her people.

This book stems from my years of activism and is based on the magical intention to provide practitioners with the tools, ideas, and inspiration to make this a better world. What speaks to you? What gets you fired up to make a difference? I hope this book provides you with the rituals and spells to support your personal causes, along with inspired ideas to help you be— and create—the change you want to see in the world.

CHAPTER 1

ALTAR-ATIONS

Creating a Home Altar for Positive Change

The Energy Center for Your Change Magic

The urge toward activism comes from deep within the heart, mind, and spirit. Put simply, it comes from love. Be guided by this positive energy—your love of others and of our beautiful planet—to effect positive change in the world.

A great way to create positive energy every day is to make yourself an altar for change. It will emanate positive energy 24 hours a day, seven days a week, every week of the year. You can, of course, refresh it regularly with offerings of fresh flowers, herbs, crystals, and candles. The love energy you put into your altar will come back to you tenfold.

I have altars or shrines in many of the rooms in my house and my altar for change is in the front room. Every time I walk into my home, simply seeing it fills me with a sense of peace and progress. Visitors and loved ones comment on it, ask about the deities or the properties of the various crystals, and often mention that they would like to create something similar in their own homes. As you might imagine, I am full of advice and keep a store of candles, herbs, and crystals to get them started.

Creating an Altar for Change

Select a small table or shelf to be the foundation of your altar. In the interests of living sustainably, I like to use previously owned furnishings from small, independent stores, thrift stores, and even yard sales. Unlike newly manufactured goods, they are much higher quality and often have uniquely charming designs.

WITCH CRAFT
Soy Joy Altar Candles

If, like me, you have candles burning nearly all your waking hours, you will need plenty of them. Get crafty to ensure you always have candles that are easy on your budget and good for the Earth. Where possible, I recycle leftover wax and reuse unburned candle stubs for the most sustainable approach to making and using candles. Otherwise, I use soy wax: soy candles burn clean, are free of any toxins or pollutants, and are much healthier for both people and the planet.

Pour the soy wax flakes into the microwaveable container, cover it with the lid to avoid splattering, and heat the wax in the microwave at medium heat for 1 minute, or until the wax has fully melted. If you don't have a microwave, place the bowl over a saucepan with warm water covering the bottom, and put the pan over a low heat for about 4–5 minutes.

While you wait for the wax to melt, thread the wick through the candlewick base, and secure to the bottom of the container. Wrap the other end of the wick around a pencil or craft stick. Rest the pencil or craft stick on top of the jar to keep the waxed thread standing upright in the container.

You will need to clean the energy of your antique-store treasures by wiping them with a clean, damp cloth and freshly drawn water. If the weather is cooperative and it is not raining, set the table out in the sun for a full day. When you bring the table into your home, place it where you want to station your altar and leave a bowl of salt on top of it for a full 24 hours.

Once the wax has melted, thoroughly stir in the essential oil with the metal spoon. Now, carefully pour the scented wax into the containers or jars, keeping the wick in the center.

Leave the candle on a cooling rack to cool for 24 hours, with the top of the wick wrapped around the pencil. To imbue your candles with even more positive power, recite this waxing poetic candle blessing spell while they are cooling and firming:

When times are dark,

Be the brightest candle.

Carry the light of love,

Carry blessing to the world.

Blessed be all.

Once cooled, unwrap and cut the excess wick, leaving roughly ½in (1cm) of wick above the top of the candle.

Gather Together

4 cups (1kg) of soy wax flakes (available at most craft stores)

1 microwaveable container with a lid

2 lengths of candle-making wick for soy waxes

2 candlewick bases

2 x 6–8fl oz (175–235ml) thick glass containers, such as a jelly jar or Mason jar

2 wooden pencils or craft sticks

9 drops of an essential oil of your choice (see pages 12–13)

Large metal spoon

Cooling rack

Essential Oils for Love, Light, and Harmony

Blue tansy oil: This sweet-smelling oil is believed to be a great agent against fighting nervous disorders and emotional impulses. It is also sacred to Gaia, the Earth goddess, and brings deep understanding of life. If you are looking for new beginnings, tansy is ideal.

Cardamom oil: This oil has a rich and spicy scent and is ideal for anyone who wants to deepen their spirituality in magical workings. Its strong, feminine energy brings out generosity and open-hearted love. Try cardamom oil in peace rituals, or for greater happiness in love.

Carnation oil: The carnation flower is small and sweet, but its oil extract offers steadiness, strength, and the energy of a guardian. It can improve communication and open your mind and heart to new experiences. Carnation oil will uproot buried emotions and help you process them so you can renew and reset. If someone has been ill, it can abet stamina, release the weakness and sadness of sickness, and guide you in your return to joy.

Carrot seed oil: Warm and deeply comforting, this oil soothes the soul by keeping anxiety and stress at bay. Carrot seed oil enhances empathy, is pleasingly grounding, and removes spiritual blocks so users become more spiritually evolved.

Cistus oil: Extracted from the flowers of the rockrose, this essential oil's aroma mimics sun-ripened fruit in the summertime—sweet, fragrant, and with hints of warm honey. Cistus oil can help you handle fear, sorrow, and worry. If you feel disconnected from yourself on a spiritual level, cistus oil will restore and rebalance you.

Lemongrass oil: Calming and balancing with a protective energy. Native to Asia, lemongrass has long been used to deter negative spirits from entering the home. The sharp and bright citrus scent can lift those who are feeling blue and in a rut. It is also a love attractor. Lemongrass oil can help with a fresh start in life.

Oakmoss oil: This oil has an earthy energy that matches its name—it can ground you and remind you of what you are supposed to accomplish during your life. It is uplifting and brings inspiration. Oakmoss oil is an attractor of abundance and highly recommended for money spells. It is also associated with older women; any rituals of cronehood and elderwoman's wisdom should include oakmoss oil.

Palo santo oil: A resinous and richly scented essence. Palo santo oil contains the benefits of protection and purification and, for this reason, has been used by Native Americans and shamans for millennia to connect to the divine. It is also useful for abetting breath, overcoming headaches, and lifting depression. It is commonly utilized in aromatherapy or during soothing massages. Choose palo santo when you need to replace negative energy with positive.

Spikenard oil: A wonderful tried-and-true stress reducer. With an earthy and woodsy aroma, this oil is great for spiritually calming its user and alleviating insomnia. Perhaps the finest quality of spikenard oil is its ability to help you forgive, let go, and make peace with those who have hurt you, allowing you to clear the way for a fresh start.

Tuberose oil: An intensely rich oil, whose sweet scent can reach all the way to the heavens and contact the realm of angels. It is transporting and can quickly raise low spirits. Tuberose oil will reconnect you to your purpose here on Earth, bringing comfort and helping you to rise above depression, hardship, and suffering. If you are carrying out magical rites in which you need to connect with the spirit realm, use tuberose oil.

Western red cedar oil: This oil has a woody, strong, and refreshing aroma and is powerful for grounding. It can be used in nature spells and works well with forest and plant deities or energies. This essential oil promotes longevity and retains youthful looks and energy. If you want to connect with Mother Earth, choose western red cedar oil.

Simple and Sacred

A FOUR-ELEMENTS ALTAR FOR A BETTER WORLD

When visualizing positive change, the elements help me to stay grounded. I keep to what I call "simple and sacred" by honoring the four elements of Earth, Air, Fire, and Water. Make a list of what represents positive change to you—and let the elements keep you grounded with this four-element altar.

Choose items for your altar that represent each of the four elements. Plants, rocks, fossils, or stones can signify Earth, while a candle can represent Fire. Fallen feathers from a passing bird or long grasses that sway in the breeze can all work nicely for Air and can be easily found during a walk in the park. Water can be represented by a bowl of freshly drawn water, while a beautiful vase of flowers can encompass both Earth and Water elements. The only limitation when selecting elemental items is your imagination!

Place the green cloth over the center of an energetically cleansed table (see page 11 for more information on cleansing). Then place each of the four element offerings in the four corners of the altar (if your table is round, you can approximate). Your Earth element goes in the north,

Fire element in the south, Air to the east, and Water to the west. Once these offerings are in place, set the green candle near the center of the altar. Place the incense in the center and light the incense, the candle, and, if you are using a candle in the south corner to represent the Fire element, you can light this now. Speak the following aloud:

*Powers of the North, bring the cool clarity
of reason in your wind,*

May it bring fresh energy.

*Powers of the South, bring the cleansing
influence of Fire,*

May it burn clean.

Powers of the East, bring your fresh wind of change,

May it blow anew.

Powers of the West, bring your refreshing rain,

May it wash clean.

*Wind and water of transformation,
thank you for your blessings.*

*Fire and grounding of Earth,
thank you for your sanction.*

Stand in front of your four-elements altar and absorb the sense of newness and possibility. Allow yourself to feel the breeze of change, the warmth of the candle, and the flow of water, and breathe in the scented perfume of incense. When the incense burns out, your spell is done. Extinguish the candles and take the blessings with you!

Gather Together

A green cloth, large enough to fully cover the table

An Earth element item, such as a crystal, rock, fossil, soil, or herb

An Air element item, such as a bird feather, flower, or air plant

A Fire element item, such as a candle in a glass votive or incense

A Water element item, such as a cup of water, or a flower suspended in a bowl of water

A green candle in a glass votive

Incense in a fireproof dish

Revolutionary Rocks

When choosing crystals for your altar, select a stone that resonates with positivity. I like to switch up my touchstones frequently, but a regular go-to for me is a pretty purple amethyst. I have also used many of the Revolutionary Rocks mentioned here (see box, right) to good effect.

Mantra for a Touchstone Meditation

Mantras have a special kind of manifestation power—the more you say them, the more they will come true. I also see the mantra as a kind of mindfulness where you constantly keep in mind the possibility of creating opportunities for good.

If you carry a touchstone with you in a pocket, on a necklace, or tucked in a bag, you can perform this meditation anywhere, and whenever you like, because the mantra takes very little time.

Pick the calming crystal with which you have a particulate affinity, chant the below mantra aloud while holding your touchstone in both hands, and you're done!

Grandmothers and Grandfathers and all the Helpers on the Other Side,

I call upon you to pour forth your blessings from above.

Our planet and her people need your wisdom to be our guide.

I now see your blessings raining down with more peace in the world.

I now see your blessings growing so all will be fed far and wide.

I now see your blessings flowing to our Mother Earth like a tide.

May all be well, may all be loved,
may all be at peace.

So mote it be with gratitude unending to
you on the Other Side.

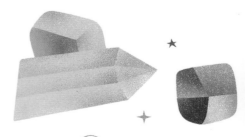

Key Crystals for Your Altar

Amazonite: An aspirational stone of hope, which also enhances achievement.

Apophyllite: A supportive crystal offering encouragement and self-esteem, which can help smooth your way through changes.

Chrysocolla: This heart stone can bring courage and will empower you in your endeavors.

Citrine: Brings joy and keen-minded clarity to help you envision a brighter future.

Clear quartz: For cleansing your aura and mindset; it will amplify your energy and aims.

Kyanite: A letting-go stone that will engender honesty, in your intentions for yourself and toward others.

Labradorite: Like the lovely shifting colors on its surface, this is a true stone of transformation.

Malachite: Absorbs and removes negativity from your surroundings and yourself.

Moonstone: Imparts gentle calm and provides a strong sense of purpose and inner strength.

Moss agate: Leads you toward your true purpose and also away from distraction.

Selenite: A sacred stone of peace that can help you hone your spiritual purpose.

Altar Plants for Turning Over a New Leaf

We often see plants, herbs, and spices such as pine or cinnamon during end-of-year celebrations and festivities, and that is no coincidence, because these natural elements are very helpful for embracing the new. Highly scented woody herbs and tree essences make wonderful additions to an altar because their bracing fragrance awakens the mind and clears the senses. They can bring about new awareness, encourage openness to transformation, and help you to embrace fresh starts.

Conjure calm with lavender: The sweet scent of this beloved fragrant plant has been proven to conjure calm and abet sleep. If you are tense or your mind is racing, it can help you to relax in myriad ways—a cup of freshly brewed lavender tea, inhaling the scent from a sachet or cloth dabbed with essential oil, burning lavender incense, or even lighting a lavender candle. We should all have a pot or three of lavender growing on the kitchen windowsill, or the deck outside, or in our backyard. When you walk by, you can touch the flowering leaves and they will immediately release a soothing scent. Why not treat yourself to a warm bath with some Epsom salts and lavender essential oil to begin a new year. Soak in all that goodness and relax into some new routines!

Hedgewitch Household Hint

Whether you buy a large pot of lavender at the garden center or harvest it from your backyard, you can cut a bunch near the root and let it dry in a sunny spot for a week. Take one of the leaves, tie it around the middle of the bundle, and you will have a stick of lavender for smudging. Use it anytime you need to clear energy, de-stress, and improve the vibes in your home space.

Basil for a blessed home: Basil is widely known as a savory herb prized by cooks worldwide, but it is also a very powerful herb for protection. In the past, basil was said to ward off evil spirits when placed at the entrance of a home and was hung in doorways to protect the people inside. Nowadays, people are more likely to grow some in a herb garden near their front porch or have a small pot sitting in their window. Basil is also a powerhouse to use in meditation or any kind of intention-setting. It's beautiful and has a delightful aroma—who wouldn't want to use basil in their intention-setting for future endeavors?

Cinnamon for sweeter shifts: Visitors, friends, and loved ones often comment that they can detect a hint of cinnamon in my home and workspace. They are correct! Not because I am baking a batch of cookies (though that does happen if you time your visit just right), but because I have found it to be so beneficial and reliable in my magical workings. Cinnamon will boost confidence—which we all need when we are launching new ventures such as activism for positive change—and bring success to you in your career, in your finances, and in your relationships. This herb will help you reach your goals. It smells delightful and is truly effective, whether as an essential oil, in your tea, or as an incense or candle—use it liberally in your magical workings and your life will literally be sweeter!

Pine for processing change: The scent of pine is bracing and helps awaken us to what is to come. It should not be limited to use in the winter because it is a real aid for embracing newness in your life all year long. This tree possesses powerful magic for healing trauma and for processing painful incidents of the past, such as loss and grief. These are important steps to take if you want to engender change in your life.

Pine can be found in several forms, such as incense or essential oil, for easy use in your spellwork. One wonderful way to add the power of pine to your life is to explore your local woodlands or nearby park where you can collect pine cones, fallen branches, and fragrant pine leaves. Gather a few items as part of your moving meditations (see page 53), bring them home, and use them in rituals using firepots or bonfires. Not only will you conjure up a marvelous fragrance, but the smoke will also release the healing energy of pine.

Rosemary for reform: Gardens, chefs, and witches all love rosemary equally and, indeed, it is deliciously useful in myriad ways. This herb is simply fantastic for a fresh start, bringing forth a strong purifying energy, especially when used as incense or a smudging stick. Used in spells, rosemary brings newness and clarity, and is brilliant for any ritual involving transformation. If you are facing a time of change in your life, keep a rosemary diffuser in your personal space to help you cope with the transitions, both those you welcome and otherwise. It also stimulates the brain and memory!

Gods and Goddesses for Good!

When using our altars, we can call upon many deities to aid in our activism. They can add their superpowers to your own force for good in the world—talk about amplification of energies! See below which gods and goddesses resonate with your purpose— a small figure or ornament representing your chosen deity will add a charge of positive energy to your altar for change.

Nereus: The "old man of the sea" from Greek mythology is an oracle. Invoke Nereus to inquire about the future, and for safety during travel by water. Ask for his guidance before a group action using a tarot deck or runes.

Artemis: The Greek goddess of the Moon is a bringer of luck and the goddess of the hunt. As the huntress, she can help you search out anything you are looking for, whether tangible or intangible. As a powerful lunar deity, she can illuminate you. Invoke Artemis when practicing moon magic and study her mythology further to design original lunar ceremonies. Enshrine her to bring good luck.

Ganesha: The elephant-headed Hindu, god of good fortune is the "remover of obstacles." Ganesha's domain is literature, and he dispenses much wisdom. Keeping a small statue of this problem-solver god on your altar for change will aid you in new business—you can summon him during rituals of prosperity or invoke him when you are in a difficult negotiation.

Sige: This Gnostic goddess is the primordial female creator: out of silence came the *logos*, or the "word". The cult, rituals, and folklore regarding Sige were held so strictly secret that we know nothing about them now. But since creation comes out of silence, you have complete creative freedom to recreate new myths, stories, and celebrations for this obscure deity. Silent celebrations, quiet meditations, and secret spells no doubt have the approval of Sige.

Hermes: Associated with the Roman god, Mercury, and the Egyptian scribe god, Thoth, Hermes is an important deity for astrologers and metaphysicians because he is credited with the invention of alchemy, astrology, and several other occult sciences. "Thrice Great Hermes" is revered by ceremonial magicians and is believed to be the wisest of all—the revealer of mysteries and the giver of enlightenment. Hermes should be invoked if you are fashioning any rituals using the signs of the zodiac, foretelling the future, or acquiring the deepest wisdom in your activist challenges.

Janus: The gatekeeper god with two faces, this ancient deity is the one to turn to when you are at an impasse or involved in a disagreement within your collective. As the divinity of January, the first month of the calendar, he is the doorkeeper of the year and can help open the doors to real transformation.

Mithra: A Persian god of the Sun (known as the "Bringer of Light") and a protector of warriors, Mithra corresponds with the element of Air and comes from a deep, mysterious tradition of Mesopotamian magic and fertility rites. Mithra, also known as the "soldier's god," is an important deity to those battling for a cause, so an altar featuring Mithra is a must for all activist warriors.

Kali: This female Indian deity can be called on to help with healing, as well as renewing courage and self-esteem. Kali is not to be feared but respected and admired. One of Kali's aspects is the Indian goddess, Vac. This incarnation of Kali is the "Mother of All Creation" who spoke the first word, OM, which gave birth to the universe.

Taliesin: A harper poet from Welsh tradition, steeped in magic and mystery, Taliesin is associated with the magic of poetry and embodies wisdom and clairvoyance. Taliesin is a helpmate to musicians and creative folks. If you are a solo practitioner and want to create a ceremony of self-initiation, Taliesin is a potent power to engage.

Call Upon the Deities to Make a Difference

The incenses and essences with the strongest scent reach the heavens more quickly than any others, which is why frankincense, myrrh, nag champa, and palo santo are commonly used for invocations.

At your altar, identify the deity that can best help you foment change for your cause—in this invocation I have chosen Artemis—and light any of these incenses. When the smoke begins to rise, speak these words to summon your chosen deity:

Artemis, holy is your name.

You are a protector of the beasts of the forest,

And the lands, rivers, and forest itself.

I call upon you to protect the tree

From the coming fire season.

Thank you, Artemis, holy is your name.

For guarding and protecting these groves,

So mote it be!

Stay vigil at your altar until the incense burns out. Your prayer will then be heard.

CHAPTER 2

SAVING MOTHER EARTH

Facing Climate Change to Protect the Source of All Life

Planting Seeds for Our Future

Activism on behalf of our planet is especially close to my heart. We are all endowed with life due to this beautiful world that we share, and we must all work on the Earth's behalf to preserve, protect, and defend it. Our future depends on this.

Growing up on a farm, I was taught to value the land, animals, and trees and to understand the vital importance of growing your own food. I followed my auntie and my mother around everywhere, soaking up much of their green wisdom. I fed chickens and gathered eggs, weeded the kitchen garden, picked veggies for mealtimes, and even started grafting fruit trees—I loved every minute. This love of working with plants, flowers, herbs, and trees, and digging my hands in the soil, was deeply satisfying and felt like a calling.

My magical intention is for our fellow humans to embrace planetary activism more and more each day—creating a positive change for every person, plant, and animal.

Sustainability and Solidarity

I recommend praying for our planet often, because the impact of climate change grows in severity with each passing season. Set an intention to be more sustainable every day, and encourage others to do the same.

Prayers for the Planet
INTENTION-SETTING RITE

The hours associated with the element of Earth are between 6am and 10am. Perform this rite between these hours, and use a local rock or stone to channel the Earth's energy.

Set up the small table and chair in a spot outside your home, in your backyard, or on your deck or porch. Place the candle, glass of water, and rock on the table to create an outdoor altar. Sit in the chair and light the candle. Light the sweetgrass smudging stick using the candle flame. Speak the following aloud:

We gather our strength as a gift.

This tribute is in honor of the source of all life.

We light this sweetgrass to sanctify this space.

This rock holds the energy of our Earth.

We offer our strength and endurance to our Earth.

We offer our love and hope for all our futures.

May this spread throughout the land.

Healing for our home planet.

I send my intention far and wide—blessed be!

And so mote it be.

Place the sweetgrass smudging stick in the fireproof dish. Pick up the rock and, holding it in both hands, breathe in the smoke of the sweetgrass. Imagine there are more trees, plants, and flowers in your neighborhood. Picture the same far and wide. Visualize the healing of rainforests, fields and mountains, rivers, lakes, and oceans, and the animals and fish that live there.

Now, arise and repeat the prayer. Extinguish the candle and the sweetgrass in the glass of water and place the rock inside your home. Put the chair, table, and other altar elements away.

Return to the site of your planetary rite the next day at the same time and whisper: "Healing for our home planet, I send my intention far and wide. Blessed be!"

This is also a marvelous rite to perform as a group ritual. Designate a ritual leader who will provide the altar elements and lead the chanting of the intention. Each attendee should bring a rock from their neighborhood. Choose a gathering place outside and stand in a circle to perform the chant. At the end of the chant, everyone should speak, in unison: "Healing for our home planet, I send my intention far and wide. Blessed be!"

The rocks are charged with the energy and power of the intention. Attendees should exchange rocks and keep them in their homes to ensure the energy of the ritual remains.

Gather Together

Small table and chair

Green candle in a glass votive

A glass of water

A rock from your backyard or local neighborhood

Matches

Sweetgrass smudging stick

Fireproof dish

Ritual Reminder

Many people have sensitivities to scent, smoke, and other trappings of Wicca ritual work, so for group gatherings I recommend small, battery-operated votive candles, which emit nothing more than good vibes and a cheery glow of soft light. They are perfect for a group in which wafting incense and burning herbs can trigger allergies. Keep everyone happy and healthy with these crowd-pleasing, inexpensive candles.

WITCH CRAFT
Intention Flags

Gather Together

2 fabric pieces per person, each cut into 5in (12.5cm) squares

Colored pens and pencils

Glitter

Glue

Pair of scissors

Colorful string or thread

Fly the flags for positive change. Craft your hopes and dreams for the planet in a delightfully enjoyable way with this bonding group activity.

Seat everyone around a table, with the materials in the center. Discuss your wishes for the world, such as a healthy planet, prosperity, peace, ending famine and hunger—anything your heart desires, as long as it is for the common good.

Using the coloring pens and pencils, write your hopeful intentions on the squares. Embellish with glittery borders and symbols of peace and love. Once each intention flag has dried, carefully cut a small hole in a top corner with the scissors, thread it onto the brightly hued string or thread, and tie in a loop to create your own prayer flag.

You can hang the flags individually, or make a visual statement by hanging them together or stringing them into bunting. Hang the flags wherever you want to see your wishes for a better world come true.

Bound by Purpose Ritual

When you find fellow pro-planet people, it's great to form a collective so you can work together toward the same goal—sustainability. This magic cord ritual can bind you together in your shared purpose. A trio is perfect for this ritual.

In keeping with the positive intentions of this ritual, use a sustainable material in natural colors—a strong, durable, and plant-based fiber cord, such as braided hemp, is ideal. Three 14ft- (4.2m-) long pieces of fabric will make a 9ft (2.7m) magic cord.

To compound the magical quality of your cord, weave crystal beads into the strands. I recommend using clear quartz crystal beads because they are energy amplifiers. Other meaningful crystals you might want to include are citrine for grounding, amethyst for improved intuition and psychic ability, blue lapis for creativity, rose quartz for love, and jade for prosperity and success in work.

As with the Intention-setting Rite (see page 26), it is a good idea to designate a ritual leader. Stand in a circle around the leader.

The leader should speak the following spell:

We are here gathered, bound by ideal.

Standing strong together, united we all feel.

Inequality, injustice, our planet we intend to heal.

Bound by purpose, with this rite we hereby seal.

And so it is.

As each member of the group takes their turn to braid, they should state their purpose or positive intention for the planet, tie a knot in the fabric, and pass it to the next person. If you have made intention flags (see opposite), tying the flag into the knot would make a wonderful addition to the braid. When you reach the end of the fabric, tie a colorful band around the braid to secure and display in a place that will remind you of your common goals and purpose.

I recently attended a magic cord ritual with the shared purpose of helping migrant families, particularly women with children. My stated intention that day was to connect these mothers with volunteer attorneys who could help them find asylum, homes, jobs, and basics, such as food and clothing. As each of us spoke, we tied a flag with a written intention into our knots. At the end of the rite, we had a beautiful and vibrant cord, which we hung in the doorway of our meeting room. Every time we enter, we are reminded of our collective values and resolve.

Make the Most of a Rainy Day

Make a Rain Barrel

Containing and storing rainwater is more important now than ever during these drought-prone times. We should all practice ways to be more waterwise so we can nourish our herbs, flowers, and garden with the water provided by Mother Nature herself. Here are some tips for creating a rain barrel of your own:

- When looking for a suitable container for your rain barrel, I recommend you try upcycling. I have some large plastic containers I picked up at my beloved recycling-and-reuse center for free.

- Install your rain barrel at least 6ft (1.8m) from your house. Locate it near the area you'll be watering the most, so it is convenient to use.

- Ensure that your rain barrel has an overflow at least as large as your inflow. For example, if the water is collected directly from the downspout of your eavestrough, the overflow valve should be as large as the downspout. This will allow your rain barrel to get rid of excess water as fast as it collects it and prevent the barrel from overflowing.

- If you are using the rain barrel to water your garden, consider using a soaker hose. You can attach the hose to the rain barrel and use it anywhere in the garden you'd like.

Drought Prevention Charm

I save every drop of water I can in my efforts to be waterwise. I try to avoid using my garden hose and augment my rain-barrel supply with water from the bathtub and shower, and with rinse water from cleaning the dishes. My goal is always to be intentional about usage, so I need to keep my rain barrel replenished! I use herbal brews to cleanse the water, which do a much better job than chemical cleansers, so I can use it to water the garden. This little charm also helps do the trick:

Water flows and flows,

Keeping my garden green.

Every tree and plant and herb,

Every flower and berry and seed

Grows thanks to this magic elixir.

Water flows and flows.

And my gratitude grows.

So mote it be.

Water Deity Invocation

On our televisions and in our newspapers, we can see the tragic impact of so much plastic in our oceans. We can do something about it by ditching plastics and purchasing recyclable products, such as reusable glass and sustainable packaging.

You can also call upon those deities whose domains are the waterways of the world. Go to a nearby lake—a creek or stream in a nearby park will also work very well. Bring some freshly drawn water in a sealed glass container or a metal water bottle. Stand by the lake and intone:

Gods and protectors of the Water,

I call upon your infinite wisdom

To guard and defend our rivers, lakes, and oceans.

To save and shield the beings who depend on these waters.

Please shower your strength and safeguard these sacred streams.

With gratitude eternal.

And so it is.

Blessed be thee.

Pour your water into the lake and bow to the Water gods and goddesses with thankfulness.

Water Deities

Brigid: Before the Catholic Church canonized her as a saint, Brigid was known as the Celtic solar goddess of poetry, smithcraft, and healing. She is dually connected to the elements of Water and Fire, and is a guardian for all animals and children, taking care of all matters related to child rearing. Brigid is also a goddess of inspiration. You can perform creativity rituals or purification rites that include Brigid. One way to bless the water you use in ceremonies, on your altar, or around the home is to pray to her to sanctify the water.

Naiads: These freshwater nymphs inhabit various bodies of water such as lakes, rivers, and springs. Naiads have the power to inspire, heal, and tell the future. Call forth their gentle energy for healing rituals or rituals that calm dissension.

Lakshmi: Also known as Padma, Lakshmi is associated with all forms of wealth and abundance, both spiritual and material. Many believe that Lakshmi can be found in gems and jewels, money, newborn babies, and in all cows. She is often depicted floating on a lovely lotus blossom.

Poseidon: The Greek god of oceans can use his might to create tidal waves, earthquakes, and typhoons. You should always appease Poseidon when you are traveling over water with an offering of olive oil; pour a few drops into the sea and you will enjoy smooth sailing all the way. His consort is Amphitrite, the queen of the sea.

Nereus: The "old man of the sea" is n oracle from Greek mythology (see page 20). Invoke Nereus to inquire about the future, and to pray for safety while traveling by water.

Guerilla Gardeners

Green Magic Seed Spell

Whether I am planting my own garden or scattering seeds in abandoned lots, I say this short spell so I know the plants will flourish and reseed themselves for many seasons to come:

Inside these seeds is all the potential;

Inside these seeds is boundless beauty.

Now I let you go so you grow and grow!

Now I see you blooming and restoring this land.

This is my tribute of love for our planet and all her beings.

Grow and grow—so mote it be!

Tips for Keeping Your Backyard Green

• Grow bamboo plants in pots and containers—they are superhero absorbers of carbon dioxide, which contributes to balancing the atmosphere.

• Avoid using a noisy leaf blower. Compost the leaves instead—you can start a compost pile in your own backyard. Alternatively, some local authorities collect garden waste, or you can recycle this waste at recycling centers. See Resources (page 141) for more information.

• Plant a garden using xeriscaping. With an emphasis on biodiversity, native plants that are well adapted to the local climate, and low-maintenance materials such as gravel, very little water is needed to produce a green space. See Resources (page 141) for more information.

• Make a rain barrel (see page 30) to irrigate your garden the natural way.

• Use grass clippings as a mulch for flower and vegetable beds. Spread freshly cut grass clippings in thin layers around the plants after weeding to fertilize the soil and as a natural deterrent against garden pests.

Be a Modern-Day Johnny Appleseed

Upon moving to the big city of San Francisco, California, I was struck by its many areas of unused land. Empty lots choked with weeds, rambling shrubs, and volunteer trees growing wild populated even the most fashionable neighborhoods. One day, when passing a large empty lot that got a lot of sun, it occurred to me: I could plant some seeds there.

Armed with only two big bags of nasturtium seeds, a stick for planting, and a bottle of water, a friend and I entered the sunny plot. We scattered the seeds in clumps, poked them into the dirt with the stick, and watered them well. Once the rainy winter season had passed, my friend and I returned to the lot in early spring to check the results of our autumnal efforts. We were greeted with a riot of color! Nasturtiums are cheerful plants with bright yellow and orange flowers and big green leaves. Their beauty is quite enough for me, but they are also edible and taste fantastic in salads.

This adventure inspired me to become a dedicated guerilla gardener and I have scattered seeds all around San Francisco that flourish to this day. I jokingly call myself "Nancy Nasturtium Seeds" in honor of the legendary tree-planting mystic, Jonathan Chapman, who became known as Johnny Appleseed. His orchards and groves gave nineteenth-century America its wealth of fruit trees with his distinctive way of paying it forward.

WITCH CRAFT
Seed Bombs

Gather Together

Old newspapers

4oz (113g) organic red clay powder (fine)

1oz (28g) organic potting soil

1oz (28g) of your favorite flower seeds

½ cup / 4 fl oz (120ml) water

A kitchen knife

Seed your future with this powerful plant bomb—scatter beautiful, pollinator-attracting plants, flowers, and herbs to become a gardening guardian of the planet.

Place the newspapers outside—this will protect the ground and make it easier to clean up afterward. Spread the clay powder in a thick layer on top of the paper. Pour the potting soil over the clay and scatter the flower seeds on top. Pour over the water and mix everything together.

Scoop up a big palmful of the mixture and knead until the ingredients are thoroughly mixed and the damp clay forms a ball. Roll out into a ¾in- (2cm-) thick log and make a cut every ½in (1cm) along its length. Roll each section into small seed balls. Repeat with the remaining mixture until it is all used up. Lay out more newspaper in a sunny area and place the seed balls on it to dry for a full day.

Now you should have a half dozen small seed bombs to plant wherever you see the need for flowers—whether your own yard, an empty lot in the neighborhood, or a spot in your local park that could use perking up. Keep the flower bombs dry until you need them and toss them with loving intention for our Earth.

Lucky Thirteen: Encouraging Power Pollinators

All plants—including those that form the basis of our food supply—depend on bees, butterflies, and the many insects that make up our buzzing army of pollinators. While we are experiencing colony collapse in our bee populations, and mass death of these vital insects, you can support them by growing these flowers and shrubs.

Borage: This flowering herb is also known as "starflower" due to its attractive, star-shaped, blue flowers. This herb is beloved by both people and pollinating insects alike—borage provides ample sweet nectar, which is perfect for bees.

Magical flower power tip: Borage lends great courage. Dry some herbs and tuck them into a little cloth bag to wear when you are going to a protest or to an action that calls for bravery.

Butterfly bush: One look at this spectacular purple plant and you can see why a bevy of butterflies will always be nearby. As the name implies, butterfly bushes are a marvelous choice to plant for our fluttering friends. They also ttract hummingbirds!

Magical flower power tip: This plant has a strong connection to the fairy world. When planting, ask the fairies to help with your pollination intentions and make sure to thank them later.

Echinacea: More commonly known as coneflower, you'll likely see butterflies hovering around these tall pink, red or orange beauties, relishing the sweet nectar. The blossoms also draw many smaller beneficial insects such as bees.

Magical flower power tip: Grind up a little dried echinacea and place it in the bottom of your shoe to bring success in any endeavor. It will also bring admiration, so try this when making a speech at a gathering or group action.

Cow parsnip: These large wildflowers, with their blowsy white blooms, can host a wide variety of beetles and butterflies as well as many bees and wasps.

Magical flower power tip: This weedy wonder is excellent for aiding transition, bringing calm and strength no matter how stormy the transformation. Keep them on your altar when undertaking a big change.

Dahlia: Dahlias are a glorious and enchanting flower. From deep red to delicate pink, this bushy, herbaceous flower is one of my favorites. They are true magnets for bees.

Magical flower power tip: This impressive plant will help you stand tall and make a positive impression for the cause you represent. Carry a bouquet of dahlias when attending a group meeting and gift them to your fellow activists.

Daisy: Daisies are beloved the world over, much prized for their sweet petals and romantic lore. This modest flower is also a hardworking bee and butterfly attractor. Most daisies have white petals that circle a sunny yellow disc, but they also flower in yellow, pink, and purple.

Magical flower power tip: Daisies heal wounded hearts and overcome upset. They are edible, so you can add the flowers to a pot of herbal lemon tea—great to serve at gatherings if there has been a disagreement within your coven.

Dandelion: Many gardeners and lawn keepers decry the lowly dandelion as a weed, but we witches know it to be a valuable herb for food, tea, and medicine—and a major friend to bees! Dandelions bloom over a long season, starting in early spring and continuing throughout the summer, and provide much-needed food for pollinators of all kinds.

Magical flower power tip: Blowing dandelions to make a wish is a simple charm that has come down to us through the centuries. If your tribe gathers in a park, simply pick a bunch of dandelions and everyone can make a wish for your collective. As a bonus, you will be planting more herbs while wishing!

Goldenrod: Late-season bloomers such as this cheerful wildflower are key to keeping bees and bugs around, encouraging insect pollinators to remain rather than move on to greener pastures.

Magical flower power tip: This hearty and brightly hued wildflower can be dried and bound to form a smudging stick, which will help you to gain insight and sharpen your intuition.

Lavender: This popular perennial plant is a must-have for attracting pollinating insects. Bees go absolutely wild for lavender, which also wards off unwanted insects, such as fleas, flies, and mosquitoes.

Magical flower power tip: Treasured lavender is valued for many properties but is also known as a plant of peace. Grow it in places where you need to create calm (see also page 18).

Marigold: One of my favorite flowers since childhood, this plant is equally beloved by bees. They frequently visit the marigold along with a whole host of other friendly critters such as flies, moths, and butterflies.

Magical flower power tip: Sacred to Gaia, the Earth goddess, this sweet posy was known long ago as Mary's Gold. Marigold is a plant of justice—harvest this important quality to keep in sachets and potpourri and grow everywhere you can!

Milkweed: Some call milkweek "Butterfly Weed" and, indeed, it can be a magnet for our fluttering friends—particularly the monarch, which loves to sip on milkweed's sweet nectar. And butterflies are not the only ones—wild and domestic bees, hummingbirds, and other pollinators also enjoy visiting this flower.

Magical flower power tip: Not only is this one of the single most important plants to grow to support bees and other pollinators, but it is also an herb that supports perseverance—a much-needed quality for all change advocates.

Snapdragon: The bountiful blossoms of this showy plant release scent during the bumblebee's most active hours of the day, proving irresistible to this important pollinator.

Magical flower power tip: Place snapdragons in a vase in front of a mirror to offset negative energy, including negative thinking.

Sunflower: The stunning sunflower is perfect for attracting insects, as well as birds that adore their seeds. This is ideal because it's important to attract all kinds of helpful critters to the garden, and birds also play a key role in pollination.

Magical flower power tip: This magnificent flower catches and holds the energy of the Sun. Bring to any ritual or gathering to bring confidence to the group.

Fighting Fire with Fire

Brazilian Candomblé Ritual

We have all heard the saying "fight fire with fire." We need to fight the fires raging in both the Congo and in the Brazilian rainforest. Call upon fire gods, such as the Candomblé spirits of South America, to defend the land.

The Candomblé religion originated in Brazil in the nineteenth century and, like Santería (see page 118), is much intertwined with traditional Yoruban spirituality, which was introduced to the New World from different regions of Africa during the Atlantic slave trade. Yoruban spirituality offers many answers to personal problems and is a popular system of aid for people in trouble. The Yoruban entities are ready to lend a hand with broken hearts, illnesses, divorce, work woes, insomnia, betrayal, infertility, politics, luck—anything that concerns the human heart.

In Brazil, Candomblé is a "fiery" faith: candles and beach bonfires are very much a part of it. You will find this delightful aspect of Brazilian culture everywhere, from brightly burning candles in the finest homes in São Paulo to twinkling street shrines in Rio de Janeiro's sprawling favelas. The beautiful beaches that run the entire coast of Brazil are popular places for rituals and offerings, and if you are lucky, you may discover candles glowing by the sea. This must be very pleasing indeed to their beloved mermaid goddess, Yemoja. Another extremely popular and powerful deity is Shango, the storm god of lightning and thunder.

These accommodating spirits are called Orishas. The shrines that you see—whether in public or private—are designed to attract and please these spirits, and the offerings made to them are called despachos. Want to protect the trees and forests? Ask the Orishas! For guidance on what to offer, and to who, see the box on the following page for a list of Orishas and their correspondences.

The Power of Orishas

 Eshu or Esu (black): Eshu has the power to bring messages, likes offerings of candy and toys, and is associated with the number three.

 **Oshun (yellow):** The divinity for love and marriage, Oshun favors yellow and should be presented with honey and sweet cakes. Oshun is associated with the number five.

 **Obatala (white):** A bringer of peace. Obatala likes the number eight and offerings of white cotton and white coconuts.

 **Sopona (tan):** Sopona is the ruler of health and has a connection with the number seventeen. Corn and beans are the best offerings to make at Sopona's shrine.

 **Ogun (green):** The best Orisha to help with finding employment. Ogun's number is seven and he has a predilection for cigars and rum.

 **Yemoja (bright blue):** Fertility is Yemoja's domain. Her lucky number is seven and she enjoys offerings of sugar cane and the syrup made from it.

 **Orunmila (yellow):** This Orisha oversees all divination, prefers candy, and favors the number sixteen. Offerings of yams and coca nuts should be made to Orunmila.

 **Shango (red):** A power and passion divinity, Shango should be gifted with fruit (bananas and red apples are best). Four and six are his totem numbers.

 Oya (white): Also known as Yansa, this Orisha is a protector. Oya favors the number five, and eggplant is her preferred offering.

Make an Offering to the Orishas

To make an appeal to an Orisha for aid, first identify the Orisha concerned with your problem (see opposite) and familiarize yourself with the colors and numbers with which they are most associated.

Find an image or representation of this Orisha. These are often available at the local botanica or New Age store. While at the botanica, buy candles in the Orisha's color—try to purchase "number candles" if possible. If you are invoking Ogun, for example, buy a seven-day burning candle, because Ogun's number is seven. Prepare an offering of food or liquor most suited to your divinity.

If you have a home altar, you should set up the shrine to your chosen Orisha there. Another option is to find a safe place outside your home where you can burn candles without causing a fire hazard—where wind, nosy pets, or other disturbances cannot interfere. Take real care in the selection of your shrine space; if it were to be knocked down, your petition is likely to backfire!

Once you have selected a special place for your shrine, place the representation of the Orisha at the center and create a circle of candles around the deity. Make your offering by placing the food beside the icon. Never eat the food intended for the Orisha. Do not make them mad. If you can, let the food offering stay there until it composts naturally.

Next, make your appeal to the Orisha through prayer and devotion. On a piece of paper, write down your true wish and heart's desire, and place it under the representation of the Orisha. Light each candle and leave the shrine so the Orisha can come at leisure. Allow your despacho offering to take effect. Remain patient and allow the correct number of days to pass before you look for results.

When the ritual is finished, you should have your wish. Do not forget about the Orisha who helped you. Keep the icon on your altar or mantel. You now have the favor of a god. Be thankful and keep making offerings occasionally to show your gratitude.

CHAPTER 3

PEACE, LOVE, AND HEALING

Rituals to End Conflict, Gun Violence, and War

Be a Living Embodiment of Peace

Our world is very complex with many in need all over the globe, and it is hard to know how to help everyone. Choose the issues that mean the most to you, that touch your heart deeply, and get you fired up to take action. Ask yourself: what is the most direct and simple action I can take to exact positive change?

Here in northern California, we have endured several wildfires that burned down hundreds of homes, leaving many survivors with nothing. My women's group donated food, money, blankets, clothes, books, and more—and drove the supplies there personally to ensure that the newly homeless received the items they needed.

When there is war and violence in faraway parts of the world, you can't always take such direct action, but you can help from afar in many ways—taking political action might be the most effective. Let your government know you how you feel, be it contacting their offices or taking to the street. Protesting war, gun violence, school shootings, racial injustice, and other social problems is very powerful—one person can make a huge impact with their actions.

Rites for Rights

Before a Protest March

I have been involved in marches all my adult life and the skills for peaceful protesting, which I learned as a young woman, remain. Civil disobedience is an endeavor that must be approached thoughtfully— heightened emotions must be avoided to prevent upset and unrest. This rite is a wonderful and easy way for both large and small groups to stay present and centered.

Form a circle with everyone holding the hands of the person standing on each side. The group leader should go around the circle, asking each person to state their purpose and intention, in turn. At a recent Black Lives Matter march, for example, the purpose and intention stated was: "I am here to show that racism must be acknowledged to be overcome. I am here because police brutality must end now." After everyone has spoken, the group leader speaks this spell:

Today we gather to show our strength

Hand to hand, heart to heart.

Today we gather to show our love

For our neighbors and all peoples.

Today, we gather here for peace always.

And so it is. Blessed be to all.

WITCH CRAFT
Supernaturally Impactful Protest Signs

I am not an artist, and my DIY skills are minimal—but no matter what your level of ability, you can make a protest sign. All the materials you need are easily obtained at any craft store. During my years of participating in public protests, I've noticed that funny or clever statements have the MOST impact. People remember them, take snaps, and share on social media. Your sign could go viral! These protest signs are also fun to make as a group activity.

Lay out a drop cloth or bedsheet over the table where you are working. This is best done at the kitchen table or even a picnic table outside to make cleaning up even easier.

Write your statement in large, black capital letters in the center of your board to make it as eye-catching as possible. Use different colors to decorate and highlight your statement (see the Rainbow Magic box, page 46)—draw suns, moons, peace symbols, Earth, flowers, or whatever imparts a playful and pretty energy to your sign. Dab glue on and around your drawings and apply plenty of glitter. Decide what message you want on the back of the sign—perhaps a large colorful peace symbol or planet Earth—and repeat the process with the second board.

While the glitter and glue are setting on the boards, adorn your broomstick with color, glitter, and ribbon. Secure it to the back of the first board with plenty of glue, then affix the second board. For added stability, secure the two boards together by gluing the ribbon in a border or frame around the edges of your sign.

Instill your sign with intention for the positive change you want to see in the world. Now, march with your sign and make a difference!

Gather Together

An old drop cloth or bedsheet

Two poster boards, approximately 14 x 24in (35.5 x 61cm), or a poster board box cut to the same size (lighter colors work best)

Large Sharpies in a range of bright colors

Strong glue, such as Caswell's adhesives

Glitter and sequins in a multitude colors

Colorful ribbon, at least 6ft (1.8m) long

A broom to use as the stick

The Supernatural Spectrum: Rainbow Magic

Each color has its own energy, which you can use for positive purpose in your craft. From candles and spells to attention-grabbing protest placards, a thoughtful approach to using color will greatly abet your magical workings.

White: Protection, purification, peace, truth, binding, happiness, spirituality, and tranquility.

Red: Power, strength, health, energy, vigor, passion, courage, and love.

Black: Absorbing and eliminating negativity, healing, banishing, and attracting money.

Light blue: Understanding, tranquility, patience, lifting and overcoming depression.

Dark blue: Change, flexibility, subconscious mind, psychic perception, and restoration.

Green: Finances, money, fertility, prosperity, growth, good luck, employment, beauty, youth, and success in gardening.

Gray: Neutrality, cancellation, and balancing.

Yellow: Intellect, charm, attraction, study, persuasion, confidence, divination, psychic power, wisdom, and vision.

Brown: Working magic for animals, healing animals and a happy home.

Pink: Love, honor, fidelity, morality, and friendship.

Orange: Adaptability, stimulation, attraction, encouragement, and legal matters.

Purple: Power, spirituality, medication, ambition, business progress, and tension relief.

Candle Vigils for Hope

Wanting to come together to share emotions and reactions is a beautiful human quality, and impromptu gatherings, often in response to a major event, can happen all over the world. People arrive bearing votive candles to show support and solidarity. Imbue your candles with more potency by anointing them with these herbal essential oils (see box, right).

Candles for a Cause

When anointing your candles for a group action or a solo rite, you can power up your candles with this consecration spell. Gather up the candles you plan to use and say these words aloud:

*The fire of these candles
burns with blessings.*

They light the way for better days.

I call upon the elders and spirit realm

*To fill these candles with the power
of positive change.*

So mote it be.

Essential oils

Basil: Brings cheer and upbeat vibrations.

Bergamot: Uplifts with optimism.

Chamomile: Promotes serenity and empathy.

Clary sage: Creates a shared mellow mood.

Jasmine: Confers a sweet and loving energy.

Valerian: Lifts atmosphere with positivity.

Lavender: Brings calm and tranquility.

Patchouli: Quiets the mind and is meditative.

Rose: Creates a gentle energy and connection.

Ylang ylang: Creates peace of mind and heart.

Orange for Hope
CANDLES TO END GUN VIOLENCE

Gather Together

Large orange candle

A few drops of essential oil, such as bergamot or citrus

Matches

Lavender incense in an orange fireproof dish

The vibrancy of orange contains a special energy of high spirits and good vibes—success, creativity, fortitude, and, most importantly, harmony. It is unsurprising, then, that the hopeful color orange has come to represent the movement against gun violence.

Mass shootings, where ordinary people going about their daily business are dying in senseless acts of violence, is heartbreaking and unacceptable. Many activists—including survivors and family members of those slain in gun violence—have dedicated their lives to this cause. But we can all help through activism, using our vote, and speaking out.

Anoint the candle with the essential oil and light it with the matches. Light the incense with the flame of the candle. Speak the following aloud:

I call upon deities of peace

To put an end to too many guns.

I ask the powers above to stop

The tragic death and losses caused by guns.

Be here now; bring with you calming peace.

Please guard our communities and help them heal.

And so it is.

I burn my candle for hours, lighting my home with hope and a vision for a non-violent future for us all, while the calming scent of lavender fills the space.

The Moon is Our Teacher

First People Wisdom Gathering

In Native American traditions, many tribes saw the Moon as a teacher, for the bright light of the full moon was truly illuminating. This monthly ceremony—like a women's council fire—channels the illuminating wisdom of the full moon to serve the whole community.

While I advise caution in adopting any aspect of indigenous culture, learning the lessons that they offer can be life-enriching. My motto is "appreciation without appropriation." Accept the wisdom that is offered and respect its source by acknowledging the person or place that it came from and how it was produced. This full moon teaching is from my friend Liz, who is of Native American descent, and whose many happy clients attest that she is a very wise woman.

The full moon ceremony should be led by an elder woman. She chooses a young man to be "the warrior" who will build and tend the fire as the Keeper of the Flame. Selection by the elder is the greatest honor because she sees that the warrior is pure of heart and perceives the good this man brings to the community.

On the night of a full moon, the fire is built, and the women of the community approach the circle crying out, "Ho! Ho! Ho!". When everyone has arrived, the young man will leave, returning only to rekindle the flames as needed. Whenever he approaches, he must announce: "I am the Keeper of the Flame."

The elder leads the women in discussion of whatever she feels is important to serve the well-being and welfare of the community—she may discuss an individual or the village, or she may tell a story. The elder is the leader of the full moon teaching and it lasts as long as she sees fit; only she can excuse women from the circle, which she does with a closing blessing of gratitude as the fire is extinguished.

In many full moon teachings, the council fires have grown shorter. The elder must know things are going well for the community!

New Moon Invocation of Hecate

BANISH WAR AND VIOLENCE

Gather Together

A black cloth

Small table or three-legged stool

A mirror or mirror tray

1 black candle in a glass votive

3 black crystals such as obsidian

6 drops of sandalwood essential oil

Matches

Sandalwood incense stick in a fireproof dish

1 moonstone

Hecate is a crone goddess and banisher of evil, which serves us well in rites of closure. Any time you want to bring something to an end—from global war to domestic conflict—invoke Hecate for help.

Create an outdoor altar on the first night of a new moon. Spread the black cloth over the table or stool and place the mirrored surface on top. Place the black candle in the center, surrounded by the crystals, and anoint with the sandalwood essential oil. Light the candle, then light the incense using the flame of the candle. Hold the moonstone in both hands, while you chant the spell:

I call upon you, Hecate, to end the deaths

Caused by needless war and needless violence,

I call upon you, Hecate, to open minds,

Open minds and hearts to end the senselessness of war.

In your wisdom and strength, please banish violence

So we can live peacefully and with full hearts.

With gratitude to you, great one, and with love and respect.

So mote it be.

Stand at the altar while the scent of sandalwood, sacred to Hecate, wafts around you and into the heavens. Pay attention to your thoughts because Hecate's feminine wisdom will instill in you the ideas and actions that will help your cause. When the incense stick is fully burned, place the moonstone back on the mirror and snuff out the candle. Record your thoughts and message of wisdom from Hecate in your Book of Shadows.

Repeat this ritual on the second night of the full moon to capture the full largesse of the moon phase.

Spellcasting for Centering

Modern life makes many demands, from work, household chores, and financial responsibilities through family obligations, socializing, and so much more—what's a witch to do? By amping up the attention to your mind-body-spirit connection, you can cope with anything that comes your way.

Our foremothers, the hedge witches and villager healers of yore, had many challenges to deal with, and few resources. With their healing wisdom and their understanding of plants, roots, teas, herbal cures, crystals, and natural remedies, you can restore serenity to your life. Their simple practices and pagan prescriptions are the perfect antidote to the hurly-burly world of stress, anxiety, and worry and the constant bombardment of negative news.

For anyone dealing with sleeplessness, bouts of the blues, angst, and stress, these peace, love, and healing rituals are the perfect combination of both mental and physical healing. These sacred self-care spells will take you from harried and hurried to contented and calm.

Besom Blessings for Sweeping Change

Witch's brooms, or besoms, have been used in spellcasting for centuries. Modern activist witches use them in many creative ways.

There is a coven of activist women who visit areas of destruction—for example, where a mass protest has encountered clashes with police. They enact rituals for peace and healing, turning regular brooms into besoms by anointing them with essential oils, glitter, and crystals, which they use to clean up glass and litter and sweep away destruction. These hardworking witches bring blessings anywhere they go.

Here is one of the spells the witches speak as they clean:

With these brooms, we sweep away pain.

We send away sadness and misunderstanding.

We stop hate and anger and banish bad energy.

With these brooms, we make way for peace here and now.

Now away with all negative; now in with love and understanding!

And so it is!

Scattering Blessings in the Wind

The mountains hold a special place in Chinese and Tibetan mythology because they are so close to the sky. One of Tibet's most benevolent deities is Nikadama, the female protection deity, who lives high in the Himalayas. Here is a very simple ritual you can perform alone or with loved ones to bring luck and blessings during the waxing moon. Spring is the best time to do this, but any waxing moon will bring fortune and providence.

Tie strings of Tibetan prayer flags (see box, below) or white silk scarves to the trees and bushes near your home or in your yard. If you live in the city, you can hang them at your door to catch the breeze. Every time the flags and scarves flutter in the wind, Nikadama is blessing you!

Tibetan Prayer Flag 101

Tibetan prayer flags come from hundreds of years of tradition, with each symbolic color representing a different aspect of nature. Monks always fly the blue flag highest, at the top of the string of flags, because it symbolizes the sky— the closest you can get to higher consciousness. Other colors include white (cloud), red (fire), green (water), and yellow (earth).

Peace in Every Step

When I was in high school, I was inspired by Peace Pilgrim, a woman elder, mystic, and spiritual teacher. She believed strongly in non-violence and advocated for a peaceful world—even in her diet, she eschewed meat and ate only plant-based food. And she walked her talk. Literally. She took long journeys on foot wearing a T-shirt emblazoned with the slogan "25,000 Miles by Foot for World Peace." Her simple approach of using her mind, body, and will for her advocacy was a great example to me.

Another great inspiration is the spiritual luminary Thich Nhat Hanh, a young Buddhist monk who dedicated his life to standing against war. He promoted non-violent solutions to conflict and taught millions of people the way of mindfulness.

His concept is beautifully simple: anywhere you walk, make it a meditation. Just remember to go slowly, breathe, and smile. This moving meditation, inspired by Thich Nhat Hanh, promotes both inner peace and world peace:

I take refuge in Mother Earth.

Every breath, every step manifests our love.

Every breath brings happiness.

Every step brings happiness.

I see the whole cosmos in Earth.

The philosophy of Thich Nhat Hanh demonstrates what Peace Pilgrim knew so well—you can show up and make a statement with every step you take.

The Cooperative Coven

Passionate people, who care deeply about the state of the world and setting things right, need to be strong-minded. But these folks, including you and me, can become fixed in our opinions and a little inflexible. The ability to agree to disagree is very important when you are part of an activist group. If everyone thought alike, think how boring it would be.

Our differences enrich our lives, even more so when handled respectfully. We may not always agree with our loved ones, but we can increase the peace by respecting their decisions and being there for them regardless.

A Ritual for Agreeing to Disagree

This simple peace-making ritual requires very little except a palo santo smudge stick, matches, and a fireproof bowl. Palo santo removes negativity and deepens our connection to the sacred. There should be no ritual leader, but the organizer can call everyone into a circle, light the smudge stick, and hold it up, while speaking aloud:

We come here together joined by our purpose.

Joined by our sacred cause, we are alighted in service.

Let us always remember not to be careless.

Let us always remember to respect our differences so words don't hurt us.

Equals together, we are united by passion, heart, and purpose.

We agree to disagree! We agree to be respectful always.

And so it is!

"What I appreciate about Lee is her kindness and generosity. She helped me out when I was in a bad way. I will always be grateful to her for that."

Political Movement Get-Togethers

Grassroots action takes time, patience, and grit. The Green Party of the United States (GPUS), for example, started out small with a vision born out of environmental activism. This determined network is now a growing national party with candidates for the United States presidency. Working toward a goal that might take years or decades to accomplish means you must stay upbeat over the long haul. What helps enormously here is the art of encouragement.

This excellent exercise never fails to bring a collective or group of like-minded people closer, and it brings out the best in everyone. During a lull in conversation (never at the beginning of a get-together), call everyone to attention and explain that you want to acknowledge your appreciation for the group. Offer a positive appreciation for each person and encourage others to do the same. Talk about a turnaround! This can turn stormy skies blue in five minutes flat.

"What I appreciate about Paul is his humility; he is brilliant but never showy."

CHAPTER 4

MAY ALL BE FED

Conjuring Abundance to Help End Hunger

Sharing and Caring
for Our Communities

Areas of drought are increasing due to climate change, and the impact on agriculture, livestock and crops, access to clean water, and public health is extreme. When I see migrants trying to cross borders, I know that a great many of them are climate-change refugees. It's a global problem—but we don't have to go far from our own front door to see hunger.

While you and I can't solve world hunger by ourselves, we can help with one kind act at a time. A great way to be a force for good in the world is to volunteer a few hours of your time. For many years, my coworker and I have regularly volunteered at the free food service at a local church and enjoyed every minute of it. The Volunteer Resource Program at Glide (see Resources, page 141) requires 85 volunteers each day to fill the breakfast, prep, lunch, and dinner shifts, 365 days a year. Volunteers assist with everything, from serving food, to bussing tables, to handing out silverware and condiments. Be prepared to roll up your sleeves and make some beautiful human connections!

I bet your community has a place like Glide that can be your happy place. What can you do in your own backyard? Where can you do most good? Make other people happy and feel your own special joy.

Food is Love

Create a Little Free Pantry

This widely popular idea is based on the concept of "take a book, leave a book" (see Resources, page 141) and the simple truth that sharing—whether food and resources, or knowledge—matters.

Little Free Libraries are autonomous—take what you want or need with no judgment or expectation. They come in every shape, size, and color but often look like a large birdhouse with a see-through door to display the books available. You can order kits to build a tiny library for your front yard (or craftier folks can create their own!).

During the Covid-19 pandemic, an especially generous librarian was inspired to expand the notion of "Little Free" spaces and turned her library shelves into a Little Free Pantry, stocking them with non-perishable foodstuffs. The food was snapped up quickly but, alarmed by how severe the need for basic resources was in her suburb, she put out a call on social media for more stock to help those in need. The idea went viral in the best possible way—thousands of Little Free Pantries popped up like mushrooms after the rain.

My women's spiritual collective and I were inspired to start a Little Free Pantry at our local church where we have classes and community meetings. We keep three shelves loaded with canned goods, veggies, and fruit, jars of dried pasta and sauces, healthy snacks, teas, and juices. One of our wise women added a second, smaller pantry for diapers, paper goods, packs of socks and onesies, and other items that moms might need but can't afford to buy. Word has spread among the community and many similar free pantries are cropping up by the hundreds.

Pay attention to what is needed in your own backyard and do what you can—the truth is, every little helps.

Starting a Community Garden

SHARE THE BOUNTY OF YOUR BLOCK

The trend for community gardens started small many years ago—often set up in unused or abandoned lots in busy districts or neighborhoods—and has really taken hold in urban areas the world over. A group of novice gardeners can transform a weedy wasteland into a bright and beautiful plot full of veggies, flowers, herbs, trees, and gaggles of happy neighbors. Here are five easy steps to get started.

1. Form a committee of like minds and diverse talents—anybody can contribute, if the passion to plant a seed is there. Your committee should truly resemble the makeup of your neighborhood. What sort of garden would the community like? How it will be used?

2. Present the plans to your local governing bodies and agree upon a site. Most municipalities have some sort of community garden information resource in place, so search for online information as it relates to your city or town. There will be some red tape involved, such as insurance and risk assessment, so be sure to tackle this as soon as you have identified a suitable site.

3. Befriend your local nursery and other businesses, such as gardeners, landscapers, or builders. In addition to fundraising and advice, a good sponsor can bring special skills or donations to your community garden, such as ornate benches to relax in contemplation after a hard day of working in the soil. Set a budget, agree a timescale, and decide on a simple plan.

4. Survey and prepare the site. Gather as many volunteers as possible—you could set up a community garden social media page to help get the word out there. Debris must be cleared, weeds must be pulled, plots may require leveling, and soil will be turned. It's all part of the fun!

5. Plant the garden to suit the unique personality of your community. Your committee may choose to divide it into egalitarian plots, but perhaps you will agree that food and fruit-bearing plants and trees will be shared during big harvests. Organize a chore chart to share gardening tasks such as weeding, raking, and composing. Most importantly, arrange plenty of community events to enjoy the produce of your shared space, from afternoon tea (brewed with your own herbs) to pie (baked with your own fruit and vegetables)!

May All Be Fed
EQUINOX EQUALITY RITUAL

Many people in this world are hungry, including many millions of children. We can and should do better. The autumn equinox is a time of harvest, and the ideal time to establish a temple dedicated to the cause of plenty for all, ideally in the room where you usually keep your altar or sacred shrine (see page 9). You can send your positive intentions to distribute the harvest to all four corners of the world (see The Directions box, below) with this equinox equality ritual.

First, prepare the temple. Move your altar into the center of the room. Place four small tables in each corner of the room and a candle in a candlestick at the center of each table. Place the loaf on the table in the East, the apples on the table in the South, the wine on the West table, and the wheat or corn on the North.

Upon the altar in the center, place the candle, sweet cakes, and goblet. Light the incense in its fireproof dish and place it in front of the cakes.

Before the ritual, take some time for contemplation. What have you achieved? Think about all you have done to feed people during this busy year. What remains to be done? Perhaps there is more action you could take in your own neighborhood. What do you need? Can you volunteer or donate to a food pantry? What are your aspirations? Write down your thoughts and feelings and your answers to these questions on a piece of paper. Look for continuing ideas or themes and make notes. Read what you have written and ponder it.

The Directions

North: The North corresponds to Earth and wintertime. Brown and green are the traditional colors and the totem animals are elk, wolf, and the mighty bear. The tarot suit of Pentacles is associated with both Earth and the North.

South: The South corresponds to Fire and summertime. Gold and red are the traditional colors and the totem animals are lizard, snake, and the lion. The tarot suit of Wands is associated with both Fire and South.

East: The East corresponds to Air and springtime. Yellow and pink are the traditional colors, and the totem animals are all birds, including the eagle, hawk, and raven. The tarot suit of Swords is associated with both Air and East.

West: The West corresponds to Water and fall. Purple and blue are the traditional colors, and the totem animals are water beasts, including swans, whales, and dolphins. The tarot suit of Cups is associated with both Water and West.

Gather Together

4 small tables

5 candles in candlesticks

A loaf of freshly baked bread (one made with your own hands is best)

A bowl of apples

A bottle of wine

A sheaf of wheat or a bundle of dried corn

A plate of sweet cakes

A goblet

3 sticks of cinnamon incense in a fireproof dish

Matches

A piece of paper or notebook

Pen

Next, take a calming and cleansing quiet bath. Once you have bathed, snip a lock of your freshly washed hair and place it on the paper where you wrote your notes. Dress yourself in a robe and enter your temple space. Light the candle on the altar and use this candle to light the candles on each small table.

Take a deep, calming breath and set the paper with your note and lock of hair in the front center of your altar. Speak this spell:

Sacred Mother, providence divine,

May your benevolent design

Flow into the hearts and align.

With shared blessings, I dedicate my shrine.

And so it is!

Stand before you altar and breathe in the holy scents. Extinguish the candles and incense, then place both hands on your heart and take a cleansing breath.

Radical Kindness

Start a Change Pot

This is exactly as it sounds: a pot for change. Look out for spare coins that have fallen to the ground, in the middle of the sidewalk or at the side of the road. Add your findings to the pot and, after a few months, see how much you have collected. Donate the money (anonymously) to a good cause—small change can make a big change for the better in somebody's life.

Cauldron Money Magic

PROSPERITY FOR ALL SPELL

Gather Together

1 tablespoon dried chamomile (loose or from a tea bag)

A bundle of dried basil

1 teaspoon ground cinnamon

3 dried cinnamon sticks

Mortar and pestle

Gold-colored bowl

Silver dish

Any cauldron can be a vessel for abundance; they are excellent for enhancing money magic. You can use a big bowl or a large cup.

Your kitchen is a great place to enact this rite. Place all the marvelous herbs of abundance in the mortar. Chant the spell (right) aloud as you gently grind them with the pestle.

Pour the herbs into your 'cauldron'—the gold-colored bowl. Set the bowl on the silver dish and place everything on your altar for a full seven days. Afterward, burn the herbs in your home fireplace or bundle them up for a future outdoor bonfire.

Cauldron of gold,

Fill with wealth

For my neighbors

Near and far.

Plate of silver,

Bring money

To those in need.

Herbs of the earth,

Share your wealth

With neighbor near and far.

So mote it be.

Foraging Food and Love

Urban foraging, or dumpster diving, has become very popular in the last few decades. Well-known proponents of the movement include Food Not Bombs, who began feeding the hungry with salvaged food 30 years ago, and The Diggers, a collective of creative political activists who came together in 1960s San Francisco to feed around 200 people a day on donated and foraged food.

Some contemporary urban foragers call themselves Freegans (a composite of "free" and "vegan") and pride themselves on their recycling prowess. The Freegan mission is to live with minimal consumption of resources and limited involvement in conventional economy. Freegans list active groups on their website, and some organize trash tours where they instruct newcomers on the skills necessary for successful dumpster diving, which are essentially: forage with at least one other person, always thoroughly check food when you get home, and wash well before eating or sharing.

Be a Freecycler

For me, the coolest of the online free resource sites is Freecycle. Freecycle's mission is to save items from landfill, promote environmental sustainability, and imbue life with the spirit of generosity, creating stronger local communities in the process.

The Freecycle Network began in Tucson in 2003, when Deron Beal sent an email to 30 or so friends and local non-profit organizations letting them know about the items he had to give away. Freecycle now has 4,738 groups worldwide and an amazing 6,690,000 members. Just think about how many wonderful treasures have changed hands and the sheer tonnage of material saved from landfill, since that first email was sent. Bravo, Mr Beal!

Freecycle's easy-to-use listing website is administered by volunteers and has the advantage of not needing a physical location. If you don't have a group in your area yet, you can start one. Once you have joined your local group, you can search for what you need and advertise the items you have to offer, from bicycles, televisions, and stereos to computers and even cars.

Offering your surplus items and finding what you need for free are both gratifying experiences and, ultimately, they alleviate a lot of stress on our precious planet.

For more infomation about these groups, see Resources (page 141).

We All Deserve the Same

Group Meditation for Resource Justice

In our large cities, an abundance of food is unequally distributed. 'Food deserts' abound with no real grocery stores or markets, where only corner stores or gas station mini marts selling junk food can be found. Fresh fruit or vegetables are rare, while hunger and malnutrition are rife. Free school lunches and food banks and pantries help, but not enough.

We should collectively hold a vision of food for all. This meditation instills a vision for equality in resources. It can be held indoors on couches and chairs or sitting in a circle outside. The more folks participate, the more the vision of food justice can spread.

We are all the same;

All should have the same.

We see hunger ending.

Suffering and poverty will end

When all is shared equally.

As it should be.

Blessings and bounty for all.

Gods Be Good

GRAIN SPELL

Many rituals have been enacted throughout the centuries to ensure a healthy harvest, from the Native American Corn Moon to the Celtic Lughnasadh. Today, thanks to modern farming practices, greenhouses, and other techie approaches to gardening, harvests occur throughout the year. At the next full moon, try this spell.

Set up an outdoor altar on a small table, with the dish of oil, candle, and incense in the center. Place the corn, wheat, and apple in the yellow bowl and set it before the oil dish. Light the candle and incense with a match. Speak the following aloud:

This is the season of plenty

When every garden overflows

And every tree branch is heavy with fruit.

Each plate will be filled,

All bellies full.

And so it is!

Wave the grain over the incense, encouraging the smoke to spread far and wide. Visit each of the four corners of your backyard and pour a drop of the olive oil into the soil. If you are a city or apartment dweller with a deck or porch, you can drop the oil into the four corners of a potted plant. Return to the altar and repeat the words of the spell. Extinguish the candle and incense. Repeat the ritual on the next night of the full moon.

Gather Together

Small table

1 tablespoon olive oil in a small cup

A yellow candle

Cinnamon incense in a fireproof dish

An ear of corn to represent the harvest deity

Sheaf of wheat (or a bundle of tall grass from your own yard, nearby meadow, or park)

A red apple

A yellow bowl

Matches

Weaving Together: Spider Wisdom

The Muskogee Creek people have a traditional story about a spider who wove a web to catch the Sun and bring it back to Earth. The web of life symbolizes the weaving of night, day, relationships, and the time of fall. This simple ritual is an adaption of their story, and the potluck meal that accompanies it—in which each guest contributes a different, homemade dish to be shared—honors the Native American tradition of bringing people together through sharing food.

All you need is a full skein of yarn. The first person to speak holds the yarn and tells whatever story they feel called to share, whether the intention is personal or for the health and welfare of the community. The speaker should wrap the end of the yarn once around their wrists, and when their story is finished, toss the ball to the next person to signal their turn. When each person has taken their turn, you will have a web of people woven together.

When you are finished, let yourselves be in the web and contemplate the meaning of your connections. Once everyone has spoken their heart, the meal can begin.

WITCH CRAFT
Lunar Love No-Bake Moon Cakes

Gather Together

Large bowl

1/3 cup / 1½oz (40g) confectioners' (icing) sugar

½ cup / 3½oz (100g) glutinous rice flour (sticky rice flour)

1 tablespoon of vegetable shortening

Wooden spoon

¼ cup / 2fl oz (65ml) cold water

Plastic wrap (cling film)

Rolling pin

2 tablespoons red bean paste

Cookie cutters in your chosen shapes

Red serving dish

Red cupcake sprinkles

At harvest time in China and much of Asia, wheat and rice are baked into big, round, moon-shaped cakes, and secret wishes or intentions are whispered into the batter. Celebrate food for all by baking your own delicious moon cakes. This no-bake version takes only 20 minutes and will bring both bliss and blessings.

In a large bowl, mix the sugar and flour, reserving a teaspoon of flour for later. Fold in the shortening with the wooden spoon, then add the cold water. Form the dough into a ball, cover with plastic wrap (cling film), and refrigerate for 5 minutes.

Lightly dust the kitchen surface and rolling pin with the reserved flour. Divide the ball of dough in half and roll each half into a flat sheet about ½in (1cm) thick. Spread the red bean paste on one sheet and lay the other sheet over top.

With the cookie cutters, cut out your preferred shapes. You can create stars and moons, flowers, or whatever looks celebratory and sacred to your eyes.

Serve each specially shaped moon cake on the red serving dish. As a finishing touch, decorate each moon cake with sweet, red sprinkles. You can explain to your guests that red represents luck, abundance, and strength, and with each sweet bite they are receiving good fortune.

Traditional moon cakes are intricately decorated with Chinese characters and are baked with a salted egg yolk in the center to represent the full moon.

Goddess of Flowers' Favor

FLORA INCANTATION

Gather Together

A large table

A large green cloth

A large vase to hold flowers

A goddess statue or
female figurine

4 candles in floral colors
(such as yellow, pink, and red)

Rose incense in a fireproof dish

4 drops of rose essential oil

Wine, cider, and juices

Baskets and bowls to hold the
offerings of food, a paper plate,
cups, napkins, and utensils

Matches

A glass of water

This ritual ceremony will help you to find the favor of Flora, the Roman goddess of flowers. Ask each guest to bring a flower as an offering, along with food to share. If possible, the ritual is ideally held outdoors.

Set up the altar on a table outside, weather permitting, and cover with the cloth. Place the vase in the center of the altar. Arrange the statue, candles, and incense in its fireproof dish around the vase. Anoint the candles with the essential oil. Prepare the baskets and bowls to receive the food offerings, and set them out with the paper plates, cups, napkins, and utensils. Ask for Flora's blessings. Speak the following aloud:

Flower queen,

Princess of the spring,

Lovely Maiden of garden and field,

Bless these tokens and fill them with your goodwill.

*May those who receive them feel your love
and bright beauty.*

When your guests arrive, ask them to place their food offering in the bowls and dishes around the altar. Light the incense and candles with the matches. Choose a guest to stand in each of the directions—North, East, South, and West—then cast the circle.

Turn to the East. The speaker for the East should say:

Sacred breezes of the East,

Bring us the gentle scent of Flora's blossoms.

Flora, queen of spring, we welcome you.

Turn to the South. The speaker for the South should say:

Sacred breezes of the South,

Bless us with the vibrant color of Flora's blooms.

Flora, queen of spring, we welcome you.

Turn to the West. The speaker for the West should say:

Sacred breezes of the West,

Bless us with the beauty of Flora's crop.

Flora, queen of spring, we welcome you.

Turn finally to the North, where the speaker for the North should say:

Sacred breezes of the North,

Bless us with the abundance of Flora's bounty.

Flora, queen of spring, we welcome you.

Ask your guests to visit the altar, one by one, state a wish to Flora, and place their single flower in the vase. When everyone has made a wish, there will be a beautiful bouquet created for Flora. Pour the water into the vase and offer thanks to the generous goddess who guards life-giving plants, fruit, trees, and flowers. Invite the guests to enjoy the bounty of food and drink, the company of each other, and the grace of the goddess.

When the guests have finished feasting, everybody can help to clean up and put away the altar, statue, candles, and incense. Make sure to recycle and compost to avoid waste. Display the vase of flowers where everybody can enjoy their blooms and remember that Flora has blessed your new projects.

CHAPTER 5

FEMINIST WITCHCRAFT

**Enchantments for Equality
and Power Potions**

Passing Down the Wisdom of Women for Our Future

I feel truly blessed that the first coven I was invited to join was a wonderfully wise group dedicated to women's rights. Here in America, women got the right to vote in 1920—not that long ago in the span of history—and while we have come a long way since then, the struggle for female equality continues. Women's agency over their reproductive rights is a political hot button, LGBTQ rights and equality are also topics of raging debate, while people of color, immigrants, migrants, and under-served communities continue to struggle for fair treatment. Nevertheless, progress is being made and the work on behalf of women and diverse populations is as important as ever.

This is why the solidarity of sisterhood is absolutely vital. While we truly stand on the shoulder of giants, today's women need to remain vigilant, advocate for ourselves, work together, and pave the way for a better future for children everywhere. Working as a group is a great boon to making change in the world—you can encourage each other, share the load, co-inspire, and work together toward shared goals. A coven determined to change the world for the better can do just that. Brava!

Women Hold
Up Half the Sky

One of my most vivid memories of activism was taking part in a huge anti-war protest, where I walked (despite a broken ankle in a cast and support boot) alongside many thousands of participants, all of us working together toward our shared goal.

My women's group and I met beforehand to make signs. We always crafted two-sided signs, to make a statement both coming and going. My sign read: "My dad is a US marine who fought and nearly died for this country. He believes this war for oil is wrong. No war for oil!" (My dad was a US marine and true patriot who defended his country and suffered multiple injuries in war—but he agreed with me on this occasion that war was not right.) We used colorful Sharpies, glitter, and other eye-catching materials, and added an element of magical ink (see opposite) as a final touch.

At the march, our little group of female stragglers were caught in a standoff. It grew more tense by the moment and the police, who were using shields and clubs to shove us back, were inches away. We were threatened with jail but stood our ground and refused to get out of the street.

Just then, some heavenly entity came to our aid as one of the policemen right in front of us read my sign. He said, "I'm a Marine" and I replied "Semper Fi," the greeting my dad taught me to use upon meeting a fellow. I put my dad on speaker phone and his deep Kentucky accent rang out as he explained: "We just don't have any business being there. This isn't out fight." The two Marines had a little more corps talk, which was very brief, but it broke the spell of fear, anger, and negative energy that nearly sent us to jail. Equally miraculously, at that moment, the police began to disperse and moved on.

I will always be deeply grateful that we infused our sign with the magic of intention and strong belief—it ended up saving the day.

WITCH CRAFT
Wishes Come True Ink

Powder the dragon's blood resin using the pestle and mortar and crush the rose petals into the powder. In the glass bowl, and using the silver spoon, combine the powdered resin with an equal amount of gum arabic powder. Add the alcohol, a little at a time, and mix until you get the consistency you require. Add the essential oils. Dip the pen into the fluid and test out on the scratch paper, adding a little more gum arabic if the ink doesn't adhere to the pen and paper, or more dragon's blood resin if you require a deeper color. When you are happy with the texture and color of your magic ink, transfer it to the bottle using the funnel. Seal carefully and store until ready to use.

Use the ink to write down what you really want in your life. Using this fast magic, you can make your dreams come true!

Gather Together

1 part dragon's blood resin, available online or from health stores (both *Dracaena cinnabari* and *Draceana draco* will easily dissolve in alcohol and are suitable for creating ink)

Pestle and mortar

2 red rose petals

Small glass mixing bowl

Silver spoon

1 part gum arabic powder (a thickener, found at art supply stores)

10 parts alcohol, such as isopropyl alcohol (surgical spirit)

2 drops of cinnamon essential oil

2 drops of bay essential oil

2 drops of rose essential oil

A pen you can dip into the bottle (an old ballpoint pen will work well)

Scratch paper

Small funnel

1fl oz (28ml) bottle with an airtight top

Brews for the Brave

The British have a point that many of life's issues can be solved with a good cup of tea. When gathering with your collective, hosting a ritual, or before a public action, I highly recommend sharing a strong pint of herbal tea. This practical magic gives both comfort and strength to everyone, and I bring a freshly brewed herbal tea in a thermos or big travel mug with me as it is always good to share a cup of courage.

Teambuilding Tea Ceremony

Bonding over a warming brew will help to resolve any disagreements within your caucus. All you need for this informal group rite is a large brew of herbal tea (see Herbal Teas, opposite, for suggestions), enough cups for everyone, and comfortable seating. Once everyone has a cup of tea, each person should share what is on their mind—the group can offer a solution and share ideas about how different solutions can work for everyone.

I have witnessed breakthrough thinking from this process. It may take a few rounds of hot tea, but you'll get there—and you will become closer and more bonded as a team committed to progress. Cheers!

Herbal Teas to Bolster and Support Activists

All these brews are pleasing and offer different benefits depending on the needs of the moment. Simply add hot water, leave to steep for 5–10 minutes, and enjoy!

Yarrow (strength for warriors): This old-time and beloved herb has been valued through the ages for giving fortitude. It was also used to heal the wounds of those who protect and defend, which makes it the perfect herb for those fighting for justice and equality. Brew a cup of yarrow tea when you are feeling drained and need to restore.

Hawthorn (equanimity tea): Hedge witches have cherished hawthorn for years for the healing properties that help mind, body, and spirit. This tea is good for general well-being but especially for preventing mental, physical, or emotional exhaustion. Hawthorn supports your heart and helps you process difficult feelings such as grief, loss, and sadness, so you can regain a sense of equanimity. Anyone involved in advocacy will encounter tough situations, and maybe even become the recipient of anger and upset. You can hit reset with a brew of hawthorn tea, which will help you let go and move on without rancor.

Skullcap (to balance your emotions): The work of activism is intense, and this witchy favorite is good for re-grounding after putting out a lot of mental and emotional energy. Upset and unrest can be calmed and rebalanced with skullcap tea. Drink it at sunset and you will immediately feel emotional easing and tranquility.

Basil (fortitude infusion): You probably enjoy basil in your cooking recipes, and it is renowned for money magic, but this is also a true powerhouse herb that has been treasured all around the world for thousands of years due to its spiritual rejuvenation abilities. Basil is so bracing that it clears the mind, fends off stress, and, best of all, imparts a strong feeling of resolve, which is much needed by change advocates. Basil is a herb that blends with other teas so you can combine it with chamomile, lavender, and any of the other herbs in this list for a cup of pure power and fortitude.

Mimosa (essence of exultation): The bark of this prized ornamental tree has been used in Chinese medicine for millennia, where it is known as *he huan pi* or "happiness bark." A sense of gladness is brought about through emotional release, which may even cause you to shed a few tears. While this might not sound like the essence of happiness, repressed emotions are a block to joy and letting them flow out is freeing and healing to the psyche. This most liberating tea will refresh you in a significant way.

Oat: Power Potion

I find it delightful that oat milk has become so wildly popular and trendy. The ancients were the first to enjoy oat milk tea by simply harvesting the young tops and seeds of the oat plant, which exude a milky liquid. This is marvelous for your nervous system—it creates a sense of serenity and concentrated energy, giving you the strength to take on anything while keeping your cool. If you ever feel burned out or overwhelmed, drink oat milk or add a dash of oat milk to herbal tea. After a cup or two, you will be able to tackle anything!

Chamomile (a tension-calming tisane): Wise women and mothers through the ages have relied on chamomile tea as a bedtime drink because its mildness makes it perfect for children. This excellent herb abets sleep and imbues a sense of stillness, but it can also lift moods and overcome grumpiness. If attitudes at your collective meeting could be improved, serve generous cups of this herbal tea and people will agree with each other even more than usual!

Passionflower (for quieting the mind): We think of passionfruit in relation to matters of the heart. While working for the betterment of your community does involves something you love—people and the planet—this herb is less well-known for being a powerful aid to the mind. It abets intellectual clarity, by turning off mental chatter, offering a calm and centered mind, and by helping you sleep.

Decompression Session

POST-PROTEST RITUAL

While most folks go out of their way to be peaceful and civil, part of the life of an activist is encountering those who don't share your opinions—they may express that sentiment loudly, or in ways that are very direct and pointed, which can feel very personal. If, like me, you are a sensitive soul, it takes a lot of effort to accept conflict as part of the process and to deal with it rationally rather than emotionally. Remaining clear-minded is key and sharing your experience with your coven and collective can help you stay the course. I have learned that it is vital to get together, to process what has happened at a protest or other public activism.

Set a meeting place or time where you know you can be safe and secure—ideally at a group member's home or your collective's regular meeting place.

As people arrive, offer them a cup of herbal tea and a comfortable place to sit. No doubt, emotions will be running high. The tea will help folks relax and offer consolation as well as reassurance. Once everyone is present, ask them to sit in a circle, then place the white bowl in the center.

Speak the following aloud:

In this safe space, we bear witness to our experience.

Our circle of trust is where we are safe to speak our truth.

Whatever takes place, we offer mutual support.

Here is the place to ask for what you need.

Everyone is equal here, everyone deserves to be heard.

We cleanse our hearts and reforge our unity in our resolve.

In this space, we honor our experience and each other.

Blessings to all; blessed be.

After the ritual, gather up the bowl and tea mugs, composting any tea bags. Scatter the salt on the sidewalk or steps outside for energy cleansing.

Gather Together

A large thermos of herbal tea (see page 75)

Compostable paper cups

A large white bowl

A box of coarse sea salt

Spells for Sisterhood

When I was first out of college and moved to the big city, I was a naive young woman, having grown up on a farm outside of a tiny town. Thank goodness other women took me under their wing and helped me along my way. One favorite showed me how to pin my wallet underneath my blouse and sweater. Otherwise—she pronounced, in an unforgettable Coney Island accent—"pickpockets on buses and trains would have a field day." I got a good education from wise women on how to live in a large city more safely, for which I am forever grateful.

Consciousness-Raising Ritual

Sadly, personal safety for women remains a perennial concern. One urban witch taught my friends and I some basic, commonsense measures, alongside the following psychic shielding technique.

This rite can be performed whenever at least two women are present and works just as well with small groups as it does larger numbers. It involves nothing more than sitting on the floor in a comfortable position and, after ten deep breaths, speaking the chant (shown opposite) aloud.

We women are the source of all life.

As a woman, I am strong and wise.

As a woman, my potential is without limit.

I am of the lineage of the goddess.

We women are the source of all wisdom.

We will own our personal power,

We will own our collective power.

We will have full agency over our own lives and bodies.

The potential of all women is limitless.

The power of all women is limitless.

We own our power, individually and together.

We own our power to do good.

And so it is, this day and all days.

Sisterhood Protection

HOT FOOT POWDER

The first Californian coven I joined included many college women and recent graduates, in an area where safety both on and off campus was a major concern. When one of the women in our group was attacked, we co-created a hot foot protection powder to sprinkle outside our homes, outside classrooms, and on paths we often used. It is easy to make and can be a proactive way to discourage those with ill intentions from coming near.

Spoon the ingredients into the jar with the silver spoon and stir widdershins (counterclockwise).

By the power of intention, this brew protects and defends

By the power of magic, herbs of protection blend.

Anyone intending ill, away we now send.

We welcome sisters, fellows, and friends.

By the power of this potion, our worries now end.

So mote it be.

Sprinkle the powder while walking widdershins around your home or paths you frequent. Speaking the spell or reciting it silently while sprinkling amplifies its power.

We made several batches, a jar for each of the women in our group, and it worked wonderfully. Women looking out for other women is powerful magic in and of self. However, I will always recommend safety measures such as a loud whistle, a handy phone, and anything else you need for your comfort when walking alone, especially in the dark.

Gather Together

1 tablespoon white salt

1 tablespoon black salt

1 tablespoon cayenne pepper

1 teaspoon crushed red pepper flakes

1 teaspoon dried dill

1 teaspoon of ashes from sage incense

1 teaspoon of ashes from rosemary incense

A silver spoon

Glass jar with lid

Supernatural Soul Tribe Spell

The very core of effective advocacy is to have a group working toward the same goal. Over time (or sometimes instantaneously!), you can become so close to a fellow activist that you become bonded by your shared purpose of the heart and soul. If you are fortunate enough to have a soul tribe, here is a special bit of sorcery to seal your fate together.

Light a white candle for purity and a red candle for deep affection. Anoint the candles with honey (to bond you together) and rose essential oil (for the sweet connection of friendship). Exchange with each other a long-stemmed rose, complete with thorns. Use red ink to write a vow of friendship to each other on a piece of white paper, and after the candles are extinguished and the rite is closed, take the notes home with you.

Symbolic Candles: Sigils Magnify Your Magic

The term "sigil" derives from the word for seal. A sigil is a magical glyph or symbol that is used in ritual to deepen focus or intensify magical powers.

Carving symbols onto your candles is a simple and profound way to deepen your magic. What symbols are meaningful to you? Certain crosses, vines, flowers, hieroglyphs, and many other images have deep magical associations, so feel free to delve in and experiment to find the symbols that work best for you in your spells. Other sigils for spellwork might include planetary glyphs, equality symbols (for women or Black Lives Matter, for example), astrology, runes, Enochian tablets, letters, numbers, or even mystical cyphers such as hermetic crosses or kabalistic signs.

Crystals

There are plenty of ways that crystals can help to amplify your feminist superpowers. For better organizational habits, wear pearl. For unwinding and simplifying, wear turquoise. To bring new energy and new prospects, wear aventurine.

The days of the week were named for the planets of Hellenistic astrology—the Sun, the Moon, Mars, Mercury, Jupiter, Venus, and Saturn—and the gods of Greco-Roman and Norse mythology that were associated with each one. While there is some debate about which stones are best suited to which day, below is a list of some of the crystals most commonly associated with each.

Use the crystal associated with the day on which you are performing your spell. This will attract the energy of that specific day of the week and the planet that day is ruled by, and will amp up the power of the ritual by invoking the deity.

Power Gems for Each Day of the Week

Sunday: The Sun (Sol), topaz, sunstone

Monday: The Moon (Lunar), moonstone, pearl

Tuesday: Mars (Ares, Tiw/Tyr), ruby, garnet

Wednesday: Mercury (Hermes, Odon), tanzanite, amethyst

Thursday: Jupiter (Zeus, Thor), emerald, sapphire

Friday: Venus (Aphrodite, Frigg/Freyja), emerald, peridot

Saturday: Saturn (Cronus), blue topaz, lapis lazuli

Use the Voice: Sacred Speaking Stones

Our voices are one of the most important tools in magic for change. Perhaps you're speaking at a large gathering, where you'll need to project your voice with strength and conviction, or perhaps you're knocking door-to-door, to speak with individuals on a topic you are passionate about. Even at home alone, when chanting the words of a spell, your voice carries power and intention.

An easy way to amplify the power of your voice is with crystals—amber, amethyst, aquamarine, azurite, blue obsidian, blue topaz, blue tourmaline, kunzite, and purple jade are what I call "speaking stones." If you are chanting or speaking in public, wear these stones in chokers or necklaces to manifest a noticeable change for the better.

The Power of Pink: Using Crystals to Influence

A ring with a pink stone packs a real punch in engendering change. Any finger will work well, but the right gem on your little finger can help you find and pursue new opportunities and change the direction of your whole life. There can be a lot of power in one little ring!

Attraction Magic

Invoking Sacred Feminine Deities

Thanks to the female impulse to protect and defend, witchcraft is inherently activist. Women working on behalf of other women is powerful magic and has helped many through the centuries. To this day, it plays a major role in defending women and their rights, as well as protecting children, underserved populations, animals, and our mother planet. All benefit from the force of women working together, hand in hand, for the purpose of change. Whenever you and your coven embark on a new phase, a creative project, or personal ritual, you are further awakening to your destiny.

Witchcraft is a highly creative enterprise and homing in on feminine energy will greatly augment the power and effectiveness of your magical workings. The nine muses—daughters of memory and rulers of creative endeavors— can help you find your true path. See the "Summoning the Muses" box opposite for a "field guide" to the muses, which will help you to determine which one you should invoke for aid.

In truth, you can call upon any god or goddess with whom you feel a deep connection. The Goddess, in all her glorious incarnations, is the supreme creative force and brings all into being. Long before the birth of Christianity, people worshiped the Goddess who represents fertility, rebirth, wisdom, and life. But the muses can guide you in your personal inventiveness. They will help to sing the song of you and express yourself through poetry, art, dance, theater, academia, music, communication—any way in which you need to reveal unseen and unknown sides of yourself.

Place an offering to your chosen muse on your altar or shrine—perhaps a verse of poetry or a drawing—

that shows your gratitude and appreciation for all you have received and will continue to receive as inspiration from your muse. Chant aloud:

O [name of muse], wise and true,

I will walk with thee in the Elysian Fields and back.

Anoint me here and now.

Thanks to you, inspiration I will never lack.

Summoning the Muses

Calliope: "The Fair Voiced" is the eldest of the muses and presides over epic poetry.

Clio: "The Proclaimer" is the muse of history, who carries a scroll of knowledge.

Erato: "The Lovely" has domain over the poetics of love and mimicry and carries a lyre.

Euterpe: "The Giver of Pleasure" plays a flute. Her sphere of influence is music.

Melpomene: "The Songstress" wears the mask of tragedy, over which she presides.

Polyhymnia: "She of Many Hymns" is the veiled muse of sacred poetry.

Terpsichore: "The Whirler" had dominion over dance.

Thalia: "The Festive" wears the mask of comedy.

Urania: "The Heavenly" presides over both astronomy and astrology.

Solidarity Shrine Spell

Attracting like-minded folks creates a collective sense of solidarity, which is the key to activism. I have dedicated altars in my home, but I also create smaller shrines for inspiration, which I change up seasonally and as needed. I recently created one to attract writers and poets, as well as invoking the muses.

You can have a shrine dedicated to whatever you are looking to bring into your life. On a shelf, small table, or even a small section of a bookshelf, gather an alliance of ornaments. Below are a few items to use that will attract people with whom you can work to co-create positive change.

Vines

Vines bind people together, so the next time you are walking in the woods and see a wild vine or ivy, snip off a small section—about 1ft (30cm) in length—and take it home. (Remember, when wildcrafting, "do no harm" and only take a little where there is abundance.) Use that length of ivy to encircle your shrine.

Stones

Place stones that build relationships, such as yellow topaz, rose quartz, amethyst, peridot, and moss agate. Several stones will represent several new friends.

Ornaments

An ornament or figure of a deity that represents the bonds of friendship, such as Freyja or any of the muses, will greatly increase the power of affinity.

Candles

Yellow candles and pink candles will enhance bonding energy. You can anoint them with essential oils, such as bergamot, sandalwood, or (my favorite) cinnamon, to add yet another dimension of connection to your solidarity shrine. I regularly burn cinnamon incense on my shrine, and I also use it when I feel the need to send a little burst of positive energy into the world.

Sacred Support Prayer to Help People at a Distance

Sometimes the daily news can feel overwhelming, but even small actions, such as lighting candles and incense at my shrine of solidarity, can help. This prayer to help people at a distant sends aid over the miles.

To friends and strangers across the land,

We send support so you can withstand

All the challenges you face, unseen and unplanned.

To our brothers and sisters across the land,

We are with you in mind and spirit; together we stand.

We call upon Mother Earth and the gods
who commend

To come to your aid with their great love
and take you by the hand.

And so it is. Blessed be.

Attraction Magic

SPELL FOR FINDING THE LIKE-MINDED

Gather Together

2 body-shaped candles
(or pink candles)

3 fireproof dishes

4 stems of rosemary leaves

Amber essential oil or resin

Amber incense

Matches

Have you ever attended a community meeting, art opening, or book reading and hit it off with the person seated beside you? You meant to exchange business cards, but one thing led to another, and now you have no way of getting in touch. It's time for some magical intervention. Try this spell and you will soon be bumping into each other at your neighborhood coffee shop.

Body-shaped candles can be purchased at your local metaphysical store. Purchase a female figure if you want to reach out to a woman and a male figure to communicate with a man. If you can't find any with this shape, use two pink candles instead.

Set the candles on fireproof dishes on your altar. Lay the fresh rosemary around the candles. Rub amber essential oil or resin on the candles, then light the candles and the amber incense with the matches. Break off some rosemary and sprinkle it in the incense dish. Hold your hands together in front of the candles. Speak the following aloud:

Sister/brother stranger, friend I met today,

Merry may we meet again, with every word I say.

I draw you closer to me.

So mote it be.

Safely extinguish the candles and incense. The rosemary in the spell will make your new acquaintance remember you, and the amber resin will cause that person to "stick" to you as your friend.

Sanctifying Smoke: Female Fire

WOMAN-POWERED INCENSE

A thurible, or censer, is a type of incense burner useful for burning more than just one stick of incense. It represents the elements of Air and Fire, and the plants used, such as raspberry leaf, ginger, sage, rose, and thyme, have properties of sacred femininity. The smoke will sanction your space, boost your magical workings, and please the goddesses.

Grind the leaves, petals, and herbs together in the mortar and pestle for at least 3 minutes, until they are well mixed. Prepare the thurible by carefully lighting the charcoal and placing it inside with a pair of tongs. Swinging the thurible back and forth will encourage the charcoal to heat up. The coal should be glowing red before you place the incense on it. Place the thurible at the very center of your altar. Speak the following aloud:

With these goddess-blessed herbs,

We implore the goddesses who protect all women

To encircle us with your divine love

And bring your strength to us all.

With gratitude and love eternal, blessed be.

When you are ready, open the top of the thurible and use a spoon to scoop incense on top of the charcoal inside. Close the lid and watch as the smoke floats into the air, sanctifying the space and imbuing your cause with the sacred energy of the divine feminine.

After the ceremony, take great care to dispose of your charcoal and incense responsibly. The thurible can get hot, so handle with care, and tip the charcoal and incense into a bucket of water to ensure any heat is fully extinguished.

Gather Together

1 part dried rose petals

2 parts ground ginger

2 parts dried clary sage

3 parts dried thyme

1 part dried raspberry leaf

Mortar and pestle

A thurible, or censer (incense burner)

Charcoal

Tongs

Spoon

A bucket of water, in case of fire

Warrior Witch Mask-Making

Reveal Your Sacred Self

This is one of the most empowering group rituals you can do, and it is immensely fun. Not only will you feel inspired and reenergized, but you will also see yourself—and everyone in your coven or collective—through new eyes. To create a safe and sacred space, keep the lights low and play music (the sound of women releasing their beautiful voices loud and clear will create a beautiful atmosphere).

Light the incense and candles. Cover the table with butcher paper and lay out the mask-making supplies. If possible, use cardboard boxes to form a small wall between each mask-making station, to create privacy and help each participant feel completely comfortable in disclosing the heretofore hidden side of her sacred self. Fix a large sheet of butcher paper to the wall.

When you are ready to begin, each woman should take a turn to step up to the paper on the wall, and state aloud the positive qualities she sees in herself in as free-form, affirmative, and upbeat a way as possible. Others can chime in with encouraging and esteem-boosting words—it is amazing to hear the unexpected perceptions of others, and this part of the experience can be life-changing. Write them all down on the paper. Each woman should take the paper, covered in positive affirmations, back

to her workstation and leave a fresh sheet pinned up for the next person.

Use the words on the paper to envisage the type of mask you want to create—they are the source of inspiration for masks of power and beauty. Draw the large mask shape on the posterboard and cut it out, leaving holes for the eyes, nose, and mouth. Dip the newspaper strips into the paste mixture, then glue these onto your mask shape, molding it to create any features you want, such as a long nose, a beak; use your imagination to the fullest. Begin shaping the mask into a curve to fit over your face.

Now, turn up the music and begin to glue on the decorations and adornments. With paint, glitter, feathers, and sequins, create an expression of your inner and outer beauty on paper. Listen to the throbbing drums and the hypnotic beats; listen to your own inner rhythms. When the masks are complete, glue a stick to the base of each one so that they can be held over the face like Venetian masquerade masks. As the masks dry, dance to the music.

When everyone's masks are dry, take turns to step into the middle of the room, wearing a veil or scarf over the mask. Each woman should announce her revelatory self. For example, "I am the Fire Goddess" or "I am the Selkie of the Irish Coast" before casting off the protective veil and revealing her "secret" self. All the beautiful, masked women should dance together to the music and raise the energy in the room. While this is taking place, the level of self-esteem in the room will skyrocket.

The masks can be kept as totems to be worn in the event of poor self-image. Hang your mask on the wall in your bedroom or office as a constant reminder of your true and beautiful self.

Gather Together

A large work table

Incense in a fireproof dish

Candles of many colors

Cardboard boxes and shoeboxes (optional)

Butcher (kraft) paper

Poster board

Old newspaper, torn into strips

All-purpose (plain) flour (mixed with water to make a plaster-like paste)

Glue

Decorations (such as paint, glitter, feathers, sequins, and colored markers)

Stick

Veils or scarves

The Legacy of Witches and Wise Women

The Sacred Female Energy of Cauldrons

Also known as the "Cup of Cerridwen," cauldrons are a mighty magical tool. Cauldrons typically have three legs for ultimate stability, rather like a tripod altar. They are very practical for mixing your herbs and essential oils but are also extremely versatile and can be adapted for outdoor ritual and seasonal altars.

Their magic comes down to us from an ancient Celtic path, where they were used for cooking, scrying, and ritual work. As a vessel, the cauldron symbolizes abundance—it can contain the energy of a group intention, or the divine inspiration of the Goddess. The round basin also represents the woman's womb, the origin of all human life, making it especially useful in feminist witchcraft.

In seasonal rituals, cauldrons can be used to hold earth or water. In the spring, the cauldron can be a rain jar or a flower-filled fountain. You can scry with a cauldron full of water and foresee the future by reading the reflections. In the summer, the cauldron can be a cup and in the fall it can be a pumpkin. A true magical cauldron should be able to withstand fire (which represents rebirth, as the phoenix rises from the ashes of the past). In winter, you can use this magical tool to burn papers on which you have written your intentions or a spell parchment and send your wishes to the Goddess upon the smoke and flames.

Honoring Our Pagan Past

Beginning with Eve, who was blamed for the introduction of evil (or knowledge) into the world, women's wisdom—the Dark, Sacred Feminine—has frightened those who don't understand or embrace it. Women who spoke their mind, who challenged authority, or who espoused spirituality outside the codified rules of any church have traditionally been considered a danger to social order and have been silenced. Donna Read, in her masterful documentary film *The Burning Times* (see Resources, page 141), explores this history of the Dark Ages, when an estimated three million women were burned as suspected witches.

Similarly, we have the Salem Witch trials, which took place in colonial Massachusetts toward the end of the seventeenth century. When nine-year-old Elizabeth Parris and eleven-year-old Abigail Williams began having strange seizures, the two girls broke down under pressure from village elders and claimed to be under a spell. A trial was convened that went on for weeks and "witch fever" spread throughout New England. Those considered to be "local riffraff" by community leaders were under special scrutiny and even those not under any suspicion at all were at the mercy of the judiciary, especially women with property ripe for confiscation by greedy public officials. Finally, one year after the first conviction and hanging of Bridget Bishop, a newly established superior court was

founded, which put a stop to the conviction of witches—although not until 20 individuals had been executed on trumped-up charges.

While we have progressed in so many ways since 1692, persecution can still happen. We must acknowledge and learn from women's wisdom, and the Dark, Sacred Feminine at its essence. Men can also embrace their feminine sides and fully express them. We remember the "Burning Times" with their torture and negation of the female spirit. Let us together express what was once made silent.

In 1992, on the 300th anniversary of the Salem Witch trials, the largest number of witches in history congregated to "reclaim" Salem. Many have stayed, becoming citizens of the town and opening all manner of successful enterprises from retail outlets to bookstores, workshops, and much more. This footnote to our pagan history reflects our high regard for our religious history and how it matters today more than ever.

CHAPTER 6

MANIFESTING MAGIC

Prosperity Spells and Money Charms for the Greater Good

The More We All Share,
the More All Will Have

I simply love the beauty and history of my Northern California home, but when I moved here decades ago, I was shocked at the basic cost of living. To adjust, I focused on the magic of abundance, and the first spellwork I performed was money magic. Money spells are among the most practical kinds of magic you can do—lifting stress away from financial worry enables you to pursue your true passions and work toward your aspirations.

The Bay Area is also legendary for being a hotbed of activism, home to equality warriors and nonprofits working unstintingly toward the betterment of all. All of this takes a lot of money, and fundraising is a huge part of do-gooding. An attitude of abundance is key to success in your campaign for the greater good and an excellent foundation for your collective.

Spaces for Abundance

Power up your meeting room into a manifestation station! If your collective has a base of operation where you can leave things safely undisturbed—an unused desk in a meeting room, for example—this is the ideal space for an area dedicated to abundance.

Magical Manifestation Station
MONEY-DRAWING ALTAR BLESSING

The night before you create the altar, leave the bowl of salt and the bowl of water on the table overnight to absorb any anti-abundance energy in the room. When you are ready to begin, take the two bowls outside. Throw the salt into the wind where it can disperse and leave no trace and toss the water in the same direction. You now have a clean slate for your manifestation station!

Dust the altar top with a clean cloth, then lay down the green scarf or cloth and center it. Place the money goddess in the center of the altar, with the candles to the left and right. Dress or anoint the candles with the cinnamon oil. Place the fireproof dish directly in front of her, as the incense will be a regular offering. Determine which direction is the East and place your golden bowl there. Whichever area of the altar gets the most natural light is where you should place the green bowl containing the crystals. In the top left of your altar table, place the potted money plant. Place the herbs in the basket in front of the money tree.

Once you have your abundance altar set up, arrange the chairs in a crescent moon-shaped semicircle near the altar and invite your cooperative to attend, each bringing a coin. The ritual leader can explain the purpose of the altar and how it will encourage the positive flow of abundance to your cooperative and your cause. People love knowing that certain crystals and herbs attract funds and may even be inspired to craft money magic shrines in their own homes and workspaces, which will further magnify the fiscal. The copper in pennies is very good for money magic by the way, which is why they tend to multiply.

Speak the following aloud:

With shared hopes, long-held intentions, and our mutual ideal,

We build the foundation of abundance here today.

With open hearts and dreams for the better,

Abundance will shower upon us for the good of all.

The positive power of money will help our cause

So we can help our community and our endeavors.

This full moon is a coin and will bring us many more

So we can share with those in need and those in deed.

So mote it be!

Now ask everyone, one by one, to place the coin they brought into the golden dish, saying: "So mote it be!"

While everyone is still at the altar, invite folks to light candles, then ask a volunteer to light the incense and use it as a smudge stick around the altar and the space generally. Novices will enjoy learning about and touching the herbs, the crystals, and all the accouterments of the altar. It is inspiring for folks to experience the shared shrine in a tactile way, and this further instills the money attraction altar with the vibrations and ideals of the whole group. People should relax and spend time together after this ritual, and chat about their goals and plans for the funds now flowing in. The ritual leader should close out the event by designating a mentee to organize the next full moon money-manifesting rite. Extinguish the candles and incense together and say, one last time, "So mote it be."

Clearing the Deck for Change

ENERGETIC FLOOR CLEANSING

It is important to begin a new endeavor or a new phase of your collective efforts with a blank slate. You don't want negative or doubtful energies lingering in your meeting rooms, workplace, or sacred space—nothing should get in the way of the abundance needed to support your efforts. Start afresh.

This organic approach is best for the health of all, as well as the health of our beloved planet. I haven't used store-bought cleansers since 2004 when a health challenge awakened me to the importance of ridding my environment of toxins and potentially harmful chemicals. I know it has made a difference for me and my loved ones, and it is a good idea for all of us to consider our precious health. The smell of a home freshly cleaned with lemons and fragrant natural oils feels wonderful.

If your floor is a delicate, antique, or rare wood, omit the citrus ingredients. Otherwise, this is a magical floor wash suitable for any purpose.

Pour the hot water into the mixing bowl, and add the mint and basil, lemon juice, essential oils, and the cinnamon sticks and cloves. Stir and steep for half an hour.

Fill the bucket with 2 gallons (9 liters) of warm water and add the vinegar and cider. Using a kitchen sieve, strain the herbal mix into the bucket and stir with a wooden spoon. Fill the spray bottle with the solution and spray the stoop outside the front door, knobs and handles, and cabinet and drawer pulls that are frequently touched. Wipe them after spraying. This is a major first step to ridding your meeting space of old stale energy that might block manifesting. Dip your brand-new mop it into the bucket, wring it out, and clean the floor very thoroughly.

When you have finished, everything will be dry, fresh, and clean, ready to begin a new phase.

Gather Together

A 4-quart (4 liter) mixing bowl

1 cup / 8½ fl oz (250ml) hot water, plus extra to fill the bucket

3 mint stems with leaves

3 basil leaves

Juice of 3 lemons

4 drops of orange essential oil

4 drops of lavender essential oil

4 drops of cinnamon essential oil

3 cinnamon sticks

3 cloves

15-quart (15 liter) bucket

34 fl oz (1 liter) apple cider vinegar

½ quart (500ml) of white cider

Kitchen sieve

Wooden spoon

Small spray bottle

Clean cloth

New mop

Create a Wealth Corner in Your Meeting Space

Feng Shui comes from China and its wisdom dates back thousands of years. It can be very complex, but there are some principles that are easy to adopt into your life. One that is powerful and simple is that of the wealth corner. Every room, office, home, and building has one, and it is in the left corner as you walk in the door.

Feng Shui Wealth Wisdom

There are four easy ways to enhance the positive money energy in the wealth corner of your meeting space or office:

Purple: Decorate your wealth corner with pillows, fabrics, paint, and candles in this vibrant color.

Plants: Healthy plants growing in pots in your wealth corner will encourage your wealth to grow.

Crystals: At least two crystals, in green and purple colors, should decorate your wealth corner.

Water: Add a moving water element, such as a small fountain, to your wealth corner to encourage the flow of money.

Growing Prosperity

Every Leaf is Fruitful

Any tree can be used as a money tree if you imbue it with abundance energy, but some trees, such as apple, orange, lemon, and walnut trees, will give you a head start. Send your tree positive energy for a healthy future by watering as needed.

A simple way to ramp up its financial fruitfulness is to hang power words that represent the promise of plenty in its branches, like a kind of prayer flag (see page 52). My coven uses a lovely, low-growing oak with easy-to-reach limbs, which are emblazoned with affirmations, including:

- Abundance Welcome Here

- Money is Positive Energy

- We Are Grateful for the Wealth of Health

Cash Infusion

HERBAL MONEY BREW

Gather Together

Kettle, filled with freshly drawn water

Teapot (a 34 fl oz / 1 liter pot will serve four)

1 heaped tablespoon cloves

1 tablespoon allspice

4 cinnamon sticks

1 teaspoon dried thyme

A fresh sprig of mint

Strainer

Pitcher

Ice cubes

Glasses or mugs, to serve

Add the cloves, allspice, cinnamon sticks, and thyme to the teapot while the kettle boils. Pour the boiling hot water into the teapot very carefully, replace the lid, and steep for 10 minutes.

While everything is immersing, visualize the prosperity you desire coming toward you. Enhance this picture with a silent prayer for what you truly need, and express gratitude for the abundance to come.

At the end of the 10 minutes, add the fresh mint to the teapot. Now strain the tea into the pitcher, breathing in the glorious aroma of the herbs and spices as they waft around you. Add the ice cubes to the serving glasses or mugs, and serve.

This enchanting infusion will provide a great deal of pleasure—it tastes delightful and its wealth-creating, supernatural powers will benefit your activist group significantly. Mother Earth is generous. Most of what we need—all that we eat and breathe—is provided by her beneficence and can be found in the herbs, flowers, and trees, which all come from her. When you and your collective give thanks, make sure to offer gratitude to the Great Goddess, Mother Earth.

Floral Funds:
The Best Herbs and Spices for Quick Money Magic

Allspice: The berries of this plant bring good luck. Gather seven berries and place in a small pouch to carry in your pocket or purse for a week. On the 7th day, burn them in a fireproof dish with cinnamon incense while making a wish for whatever you want.

Basil: Basil is a major herb of abundance as well as of love. Drop a few fresh basil leaves on the floor of your kitchen, sweep them out of your home with your magical broom, and speak this charm: "Scarcity is out the door; no longer will I be poor. Health and wealth, be here now. Harm to none, so mote it be."

Cinnamon: Known as the "sweet money spice," cinnamon is delightfully scented, a bringer of luck, and will make a business more prosperous. Sprinkle a dash of powdered cinnamon on the threshold of your front door, store, or business and watch the wealth walk in!

Cloves: A spice of good fortune, which can help in gambling. Cloves bring people together and bind them. If you need to turn your luck around, use cloves in spellwork as an herbal element or in incense or potpourri to foment abundance energy.

Ginger: The root of this plant can speed up any magic. Grind dried ginger root into powder and add to your money attraction spells to bring funds much earlier. Ginger tea brings money your way, briskly!

Nutmeg: Another spice beloved by gamesmen and gamblers. Carry a whole nutmeg in your pocket and your luck will improve on the same day.

Thyme: A common herb that will attract money to your home. Each time you cook with thyme, you are drawing abundance and wealth toward you. Drink thyme tea for a quick fortune turnaround and fast money magic with this spell: "It is time for money to come my way; good luck is mine. Money thyme is mine with blessings for all."

Treasure Tonic

HEALTH AND WEALTH CHAI

Gather Together

2 tablespoons turmeric

1 tablespoon ground cinnamon

2 teaspoons ground ginger

1 teaspoon ground cardamom

1 teaspoon black pepper

Heatproof pan

4 cups / 34 fl oz (1 liter) water

4 cups / 34 fl oz (1 liter) almond milk (or any kind of milk you like such as oat milk or dairy)

Strainer

Mugs, to serve

Have you ever seen a small dish of seeds in the entryway of an Indian restaurant or Middle Eastern café? That is cardamom and it is not only there to sweeten the breath—it has been considered through the centuries as advantageous to eat before business meetings as it will freshen the mind, bring you good luck, and bestow financial gain.

This spicy herb is one of the key elements in this lovely libation chai, a great fall or winter adaptation of the classic chai recipe, beloved for its warm deliciousness that is so bracing and comforting—plus it's a really pretty color, redolent of abundance. This chai is another excellent beverage to serve at fund-raisers or at group meetings involving treasury matters because it is an energetic magnet for money. It is also anti-inflammatory and very beneficial to health.

Put all the spices into a saucepan with the water and milk and bring to a boil. Lower the heat and simmer for about 30 minutes. Strain and enjoy. Equally delightful variations to try include adding clove, nutmeg, cacao, star anise, or chicory, to taste.

Share this blend at a meeting regarding the finances of your collective. It will help grow your funds in a most pleasant way and the more you drink together, the more your funds will appear.

More Plants and their Magical Manifesting Properties

See also Floral Funds: The Best Herbs and Spices for Quick Money Magic (page 105).

Blackberry: Always use blackberry when casting money spells as it contains properties of abundance. Blackberry can also be used for protection—to protect your health and to protect yourself from negative energy.

Catnip: This magical plant is a magnet for luck!

Chamomile: Many witches rely upon this cherished herb in their money spells. Utilized well, chamomile creates abundance. To remove a curse, a spell, or negative feeling, steep chamomile in warm water, then sprinkle with basil and drink.

Cinquefoil: To attract cash quickly, try placing a small pouch of cinquefoil under your pillow as you sleep.

Elder: This plant emanates a powerful and protective energy. Plant a tree in your kitchen garden or in a large pot on your porch, keep a bunch of elderflowers in a vase on your windowsill, or carry a small bag of elderberries in your pocket for prosperity.

Fennel: Potent and fragrant, fennel protects from hexes and is a lucky plant. Grow in your garden around windows and doorways for home and financial security, or carry some with you for protection.

Hawthorn: This plant attracts the wee ones into your garden—not only pollinating bees and insects, but also enticing fairies. Growing hawthorn draws small creatures of all kinds that bring gifts into your life.

Hazel: The twigs and nuts of this tree are especially fortunate for female prosperity and protect property.

Hibiscus: The flowers of the lovely hibiscus shower both love and good fortune into your life.

Marigold: Before you represent your collective or take part in an important negotiation, bathe in a hot bathtub with marigolds in the water to bring success and optimal results.

Oak: Place acorns on your windowsill during a full moon to draw money to you.

Sunflower: The sunflowers in your garden are filled with the energy of the Sun—bring them into your home for good luck and a lightness of spirit.

Raising Funds Rapidly

These days, we sometimes feel called to help people on the other side of the world who are in dire need of money for basics such as food, shelter, and safety. There are myriad ways to donate and ensure the financial help reaches the people who need it most.

Sending Abundance from Afar

In addition to donating money, my coven and I perform rituals to create a flow of funds to woman and children experiencing displacement, hunger, and devastation, such as migrant mothers at borders, moms forced to escape war zones with their young, those displaced by climate change after hurricanes and floods, as well as victims of earthquakes and tsunamis. Speak this prayer aloud:

Great Mother,

We ask you to help other mothers

Who are suffering and need help.

They need food, shelter, clothing, money.

Your kindness can provide and protect

*These families as they seek peace
and relief.*

*We call upon your kindness
to all mothers*

*So they are safe in the shelter
of your love.*

*Like rainfall, pour your beneficence
to these people.*

So mote it be.

Pots of Plenty

LUCKY 13 GROUP RITUAL

When you need to raise funds rapidly, a simple glass pot can become a cauldron—perform this pot of plenty ritual to fill the cauldron with prosperity and fill the coffers of your organization with cash. Best performed by 13 people as a group rite, all present should fill the pot with intentional ideas as well as the elements of enchantment.

Place the brown paper square at the center of the table. The brown square will be a solid, grounding foundation for your enterprise. Next, put the glass jar and green plate on the square and place the ritual elements—the coins, the pyrite, string, sugar, and bay leaves—on the green plate.

Ask each person, one by one, to place a coin at the bottom of the jar. Put the pyrite in the jar, in the middle of the coins, where it will act as a lodestone, drawing abundance into the jar. Tie the green string around the jar to bind the money to your group and to your cause. Now, put the still-sealed sugar packets in the jar, which, like honey, are sweet attraction magic. Lastly, before closing the lid, put the bay leaves in the jar. This goddess-blessed herb has been prized for its prosperity potency since ancient Greco-Roman times.

Now the pot of plenty is ready to draw plenitude toward the efforts of your collective. Finally, place the clover, a symbol of luck, on the green dish beside the pot. Always remember that gratitude goes hand in hand with abundance, and greatly pleases the gods.

Gather Together

Square sheet of brown paper

A small table (or use your manifestation station, see pages 98–99)

Large glass jar with lid

A large green plate

13 coins

A chunk of pyrite

13in (33cm) length of green string

3 packets of white sugar

13 bay leaves

1 clover leaf

Jumpstart Your Kickstarter

MONEY BAG CHARM

Any endeavor your collective undertakes to raise funds can be augmented by this easy and effective enchantment. The instructions below will make one prosperity pouch, but if everyone in your collective crafts up their own little money bag in a group rite, the manifestation will be multiplied. Collect your favorite coins for this charm, perhaps foreign currency from your travels, which can be colorful and have real visual appeal. The coins you pick up on your journeys also symbolize freedom and expansion.

First, set up the elements on your altar (see pages 14–15) or manifestation station (see pages 98–99) by placing the crystals in the green dish and arranging the dish, bag, pieces of vanilla stick, and coins in front of the candle. Place the incense between the dish and the candle. Anoint the green candle with the vanilla essential oil. Vanilla brings abundance and is a money-magic go-to, alongside cinnamon. Now, light the candle and the incense. While these burn, repeat your affirmation for increased wealth for your enterprise. Affirm all the good works that can be achieved, and how every cent can be used to make progress toward your goals.

Speak the following aloud:

Generous spirits, fill this sack

With many coins so we can give back,

Our group shall know never lack,

Our accounts will always be in the black.

We thank you, generous spirits, for all you give.

And so it is! Blessed be thee!

Hold each crystal one by one as you visualize the flow of extra capital heading your way. Put the vanilla pieces in the pouch, followed by the crystals and the coins.

When all the magical elements are in the bag, pull the strings tight to seal it, then place (with all the magical elements inside) in the green dish. Repeat the words of the spell before you extinguish the candle and incense.

Now place the bag in your pocket and keep it there for the rest of the day. On the following day, you'll see the first sign of abundance.

Gather Together

3 green crystals, such as jade, peridot, or turquoise

A green dish or shallow, wide bowl

1 small, green drawstring cloth bag

1 vanilla stick, cut into 3 pieces

3 coins

Vanilla incense in a fireproof dish

A new green candle

3 drops of vanilla essential oil

Matches

Kitchen Witchery and Fundraising Activism

Non-profit organizers and activist groups need to raise money for their good works and are always looking for creative ways to fundraise. Bake sales and craft sales are not only some of the most effective kinds of fundraising, but they bring the community together, and can even be a good way to recruit new members and volunteers to the collective cause.

Kitchen witches bring a whole new level of supernatural, money-attraction action to the venerable bake sale. Sweet treats and homemade goodies can be prepared and eaten with money in mind and—used in conjunction with prosperity spells—can be filled with money magic.

Fundraising Foods

Cupcakes, crumbles, banana breads, berry pies, and so much more can help build a solid foundation for a group devoted to change—and create much happiness! Witches in a hurry can use store-bought cake mixes. Look out for vanilla flavors and ingredients, which have a lot of good manifesting energy.

When creating income for your organization, consider these tried-and-true foods to include in your treats. All are excellent for manifesting money:

- Apples
- Bananas
- Beans
- Berries
- Cacao

- Legumes
- Nuts
- Oranges
- Seeds
- Tomatoes

Slice of Abundance Chocolate Cake

For delicious do-good goodies, indulge in foods that carry the energy of money. Bring extra magic to your cause by making this sweet treat with the energy of money magic.

Preheat your oven to 375°F (190°C / 170°C fan). Butter the base and sides of the cake pan.

Mix the butter, sugar, eggs, flour, and drinking chocolate with an electric mixer, or beat together with a wooden spoon in a large mixing bowl. Set aside a teaspoonful of the chocolate chips, then throw in the walnuts and the remainder of the chocolate chips. Use the wooden spoon to mix by hand, widdershins, three times. As you stir the mixture, think of money, opulence, and abundance.

Pour the cake mix into the cake pan and pop it into the oven for 25 minutes, or until a skewer inserted into the center of the cake comes out clean. Leave to cool in the pan for 10 minutes, then turn out onto a cooling rack to cool completely.

When you taste the cake, think of abundance. Visualize the funds flowing toward your group and the smile on everyone's face as they enjoy this enchanting delight. For extra decadence, there are endless variations of cupcakes and frosting you can use that will bring a lot of happiness to customers and to your collective (see Fundraising Foods, opposite), or serve with whipped cream and strawberries. Money magic can bring a lot of sweetness all around!

Gather Together

Cake pan that serves 6

2½oz (75g) butter

1½ cups / 10½oz (300g) superfine (caster) sugar

3 eggs

Heaping cup / 5oz (140g) self-rising flour

½ cup / 2½oz (70g) drinking chocolate

An electric mixer or large mixing bowl (optional)

Wooden spoon

¼ cup / 1oz (28g) chopped walnuts

¼ cup / 1½oz (42g) chocolate chips

Cooling rack

CHAPTER 7

RITUALS FOR RECLAIMING

Witches as Activists for Social Justice

Changing the World for the Better
Through Peaceful Protest

Ritual work can change the world. In the past, legendary activists, such as Mahatma Gandhi, Reverend Martin Luther King, and Nelson Mandela have used ritual fasting, chanting, and gospel singing to peacefully protest, further their revolutionary goals, and change the world in dramatic ways.

In recent years, Wicca and other previously suppressed traditions of witchcraft are becoming more popular. The rituals, rites, and ceremonies performed are like works of art—they can be subversive but have a moral code and personal responsibility of their own, strength to move the human spirit, and the ability make a positive change in our world.

Reclaiming Witchcraft

The Three Principles of Wicca

For centuries, hierarchical institutions have waged war on witches and other pagan groups. It is truly tragic that peaceful, nature-based, spiritual folks, such as healers who only sought to care for their neighbors, were subject to inquisitions, witch hunts, and execution. It is a dark legacy, but it is part of our human history, and we must learn from it.

We modern pagans owe much to the witches of the twentieth century, such as Gerald Gardner, the "Father of Wicca," whose coven spread from the forests of 1930s England to bucolic Australia and the United States in the late 1950s and '60s. They formed their own code of ethics—the principles of Wicca, outlined below—and worked unstintingly to educate, enlighten, and remove the stigma of witchcraft. Their positive action was a revolution, for which we should all be deeply grateful. Blessed be they who came before and paved the path for all of us.

The Wiccan Rede

This rede, or wise teaching, gives the individual freedom to do as she or he sees fit, provided it does not affect anybody negatively. Witchcraft—especially ritual and spellwork—has wide-ranging powers to affect everyone and everything, so while you pursue your own interests, think carefully about how your actions could affect others. This tenet requires real awareness to assess all the possible physical, spiritual, emotional, and psychological consequences that can result from ritual work.

The Threefold Law

The principle "what you do comes back to you threefold" is much like the Buddhist principle of karma and is a great guideline for life generally. Negativity comes back to you three times over, so attention to your thoughts and attitude is absolutely essential. The flip side of this law is that the positivity will come back to you threefold as well, so kindness, love, and generosity are all magnified. Send good works and helpful intentions out to others—for example, in ritual work for long-distance healing, global peace, the environment, or world hunger—and you will also benefit.

The Golden Rule

The rede "do unto others as you would have them do unto you" bestows personal responsibility at the highest level. In other words, the "right action" is up to you, and is of utmost importance. People may find it amazing that both Christians and many pagans share this same moral principle, but it is vital to respect the diversity of religions. Do not judge, in the same way that you do not wish to be judged. These simple guidelines are universal in nature—they apply to any walk of life or spiritual practice. If you guard your thoughts, intentions, and actions with the well-being of others in mind, you should be a happy, highly accountable ritualist.

For anyone wishing to learn more about wiccan philosophy and join in with a likeminded community, see Resources (page 141) for more information.

"An ye harm none, do as ye will."

Gerald Gardner, *The Meaning of Witchcraft* (1959)

Invoking Guardians of Freedom

The Spirits of Santería

Commemorating Abraham Lincoln's Emancipation Proclamation of 1862 is an excellent opportunity to celebrate freedom from oppression. Despite incredible odds, African religions such as Yoruba have survived the Atlantic slave trade, and formed the basis for a number of religions in the New World. When enslaved Africans reached the Catholic lands of Central and South America, these elements blended to make an interesting new religion called Santería. African deities were blended with Catholic saints in the form of Orishas, or spirit guardians, similar to those honored in Candomblé (see page 39). Practitioners of Santería believe that everyone has one Orisha as a guardian throughout his or her life.

Orisha Guardians

Aganyu: This volcano god corresponds to Saint Christopher. His mother is Yemmu and he is the father of Shango. He can protect you from harm, but only if you make your appeal through Shango.

Babalú-Aye (or Obalúayé): This deity, associated with Saint Lazarus, can be turned to for healing. He is one of the most beloved and needed of all the Orishas. Babalú-Aye travels with a bag of corn, offering healing and prosperity.

Eleggu: A trickster who creates bewilderment in his wake, Eleggu corresponds to Saint Anthony. He is "all-knowing" and wants to be acknowledged before any other Orisha. Because order comes from chaos, it is believed that Eleggua brings us into wholeness.

Obatala: A deity of both genders who corresponds to Our Lady of Mercy. He is a bringer of peace and purity, as evidenced by his white robes. Obatala teaches temperance and can help us control obsessive thoughts, such as anger, worry, and fear.

Ochosi: This woodland-dwelling god, who corresponds to Saint Norbert, protects hunters, is a healer, and helps with legal issues. Ochosi is the Orisha to turn to if you need to relocate.

Ogun: The warrior Orisha, corresponding to Saint Peter. He holds all metals under his domain. Call on Ogun when you need employment or protection.

Orunmila: The Orisha of fate corresponds to Saint Francis of Assisi. He is "one who lives both in heaven and on earth," and since he holds all our fates in his hands, he can help us improve our destiny.

Oshun: A river goddess who corresponds to Our Lady of Charity. She is the Santerían Venus and looks after affairs of the heart— love, marriage, and money. She gives us joy and abundance.

Oya: A deity of the dead, who corresponds to Saint Teresa. She is also a goddess of the winds and boundaries. Oya is a warrior and offers protection against death and is quite aggressive. She is married to Shango.

Shango (or Changó): A male god who corresponds to Saint Barbara, Shango holds major power. Red-coated and covered with cowry shells, Shango is the hot Orisha of fire and lightning and he loves the good life, women, food, drinking, and dancing. Call on Shango when you need passion in love.

Yemoja: This patroness of pregnancy corresponds to Our Lady of Regia. She is a goddess of the Moon and the ocean, Yemoja is one of the most popular Orishas and is always depicted as a gorgeous goddess who helps girls make the passage to womanhood.

Casting the Sacred Circle

Native American culture honors and respects ancestors as guiding spirits. This Native American-inspired ritual invokes your ancestors as your guides.

Before casting the sacred circle, prepare yourself and your space by cleansing and smudging the area.

To cast the sacred circle, use a wand or your hand to mark off a circle at least 9ft (2.7m) in diameter. You may choose to speak the invocation given here (see box, opposite) and use a drum (see page 127) or rattle (see page 123).

Once you have created the sacred circle, you may call for a vision, pray for guidance, pray for healing, or choose to give thanks. This is a circle of light where you are connected to the divine source of love and light. Enjoy your journey.

When you have completed your mission within the circle, close the circle by giving thanks to all who came to guide you, guides and totems, and all the energies of the directions (North, South, East, and West).

Calling the Four Directions

Grandmothers and Grandfathers, please come and create the sacred circle of light. Surround me in a circle of light. Thank you.

Grandmothers and Grandfathers of the North, I thank you for coming and I welcome the energy of the North, Great Spirit, the sacred Mountains, connection to our ancestors and the elders, and connection to our knowing, remembering, and our wisdom. I welcome White Buffalo here. Aho!

Grandmothers and Grandfathers of the East, thank you for coming, and I welcome the energy of the East, the golden doorway that leads to all levels of awareness and understanding. I connect to the rising sun, to the warmth of the Sun, to new beginnings, to illumination, and to the light, for mental clarity. I welcome the spirit seeds of new ideas and the male energy to move forward. I welcome the energy of Eagle here. Aho!

Grandmothers and Grandfathers of the South, I welcome you and thank you for coming. I welcome the energies of the South, innocence and play and coming into the world from our child's wonder, our authentic self. I welcome the balance of lightheartedness. I welcome the energy of Coyote here. Aho!

Grandmothers and Grandfathers of the West, welcome. I give thanks to the energies of the West, the place of letting go of what no longer serves us, the place of diving deep into the void, the darkness, Great Mystery, the place of the creative feminine and looking within. I welcome Bear here. Aho!

Grandmothers and Grandfathers of the Above World, I welcome you and the energies of Father Sky, the Cosmos, Star Beings, Light Beings, Ascended Masters, Angels, Archangels, and all who work with us from the light. Welcome. Aho!

Grandmothers and Grandfathers of the Below World, Great and Mother Earth, we welcome your mud, your beauty, and all our ancestors of the earth, the mineral kingdom, plant kingdom, animal kingdom, all creatures, and our relatives. We give thanks to you and all your vibrations and your wisdom. I welcome the nature spirits and align with the elements. Aho!

Grandmothers and Grandfathers at the Center of all being, we welcome you. I welcome the energy of love and well-being, the place that connects us all at heart. May we know our oneness and our unique gifts. Aho!

Power to the People

If you are feeling a bit overwhelmed by all the woes of the world and in need of encouragement and fellowship, these rites and spells are a marvelous way to "reset."

Solidarity Smoke

SPELLCASTER SMUDGING RITE

Gather Together

A fire-safe vessel, such as a fireplace or outdoor firepot

Sage bundle

Several pieces of paper and a pen

This sacred smoke spell will help you regain your footing and feel grounded, find your purpose and forge a new path for yourself and others, and create community energy with ceremonial smoke.

Light a fire in your fire-safe vessel, light the sage bundle, and smudge the area well. Sit by the fire and relax.

Think about the challenges you face and need to overcome in your life. Write each issue that comes up for you on a separate piece of paper. Then, with clear intention, place each paper on the fire.

After a moment of silent meditation, write your hopes for the future on a fresh sheet of paper. Fold the paper and place it in your purse or wallet to carry with you. Your vision for the future will take on a life of its own.

End the ritual with another sage smudging and make sure the fire is completely out before you go back inside. You should perform this rite at least once a year.

WITCH CRAFT
How to Make a Ceremonial Gourd Rattle

Through the years, many of the groups I have belonged to have been brought to order with the help of a shamanic rattle. This vegan rattle is made from a dried gourd—choose a gourd with a bulbous shape and a long stem still attached to the round bulb. I recommend crafting a few gourd rattles at the same time, so you can gift one to each member of your collective to use.

Carefully dip your gourd into a pot of hot water and start cleaning the outer surface. Use the pan scourer to gently but firmly remove any moldy spots from the surface. Dip the cleaned gourd into the vinegar solution and place it on a clean cloth in a sunny spot. Leave the gourd to dry for a month to allow it to "cure."

Once the gourd looks completely dry, pick it up by the stem and give it a shake. If you can hear the rattle of the dried seeds inside, your gourd is cured.

You can decorate the outside of your gourd rattle. Sketch the design in pencil on your gourd rattle first, so you have an outline to follow, then paint with bright colors. Although you can use oil-based paint, acrylic paints are much more convenient and easier to clean up.

These rattles raise the vibrations in a room—form a circle with multiple participants to shake their rattles and raise powerful positive energy!

Gather Together

Gourd

Pan scourer

Vinegar solution (a blend of 1 part vinegar, 1 part water)

Clean cloth

Acrylic paint, in bright colors

One Moon for All Humankind

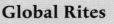

Global Rites

Do you gaze up at the night sky in wonder? I know I do nearly every night.

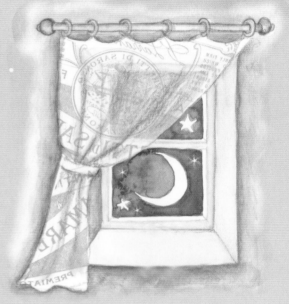

It may well be that no other celestial object is as revered as the Moon. Aside from the Sun, our brightest star and the source of life, the Moon is the single, most important light in our sky. Magical and majestic, mysterious and reflective, she rules the ocean tides, the crops in our fields, and our moods and emotions.

Since prehistory, we have looked into the night sky for inspiration from the divine. Every culture in the world, both past and present, has moon lore, myths, rites, and a great respect for our favorite "night light." The early Babylonians called the Moon "the boat of life," while the Taoist Chinese believed the Moon was a white dragon. Some cultures consider the Moon to be male and the Sun female. For example, the Japanese honored the Sun goddess Amaterasu and her brother, the moon god Tsukiyomi. A most unusual perspective came from the usually reasonable Plutarch, who theorized that girls grew into women as a result of a female essence that came down from the Moon. To this day, modern Pagans "draw down the moon" in some rituals. The very name of our galaxy, the Milky Way, comes from the mythical white cow that jumped over the Moon. A common and beloved ritual—baking, decorating, and eating a birthday cake—is descended from the Greek custom of celebrating the monthly birthday of the moon goddess Artemis with full-moon cakes. In Asia, it is said that the Moon is the mirror that reflects everything in the world.

New Moon, New Initiatives

The new moon is a wonderful opportunity for personal improvement and transformation, whether spiritual or health-related, like practicing yoga or beginning a new diet. The new moon has great advantages for healing. This phase is also marvelous for rituals that draw something to you. Rituals and charms commenced in the new moon can have tangible results by the next new moon. Divinatory rituals performed during the new moon can also bring great clarity.

Activist Naming Ceremony
NEW MOON GATHERING

Gather Together

A fire-safe vessel, such as a fireplace or outdoor firepot

Pipe, filled with dried chicory or other dried herbal tea

Face paint

A headdress and decorations such as feathers and beads

Drums (see opposite) and rattles (see page 123)

Gather together your tribe and form a seated circle around the fire.

Honor the new activist member with "growing up stories"—tales of courage, honesty, and generosity that show the best qualities of the new member.

After story time, perform the "blessing of smoke" by lighting the pipe and passing it around the circle. If preferred, you can pass the unlit pipe around for symbolic significance only.

Announce the new name, along with the explanation of the name. For example, "I name you 'Moon Warrior' because you are wise and reflective, because you shine."

The tribe should welcome the newly christened activist witch by taking turns to speak their blessing, and finish with the collective's mission: "May you see the world and find the place that speaks most deeply to your heart." When everyone around the circle has spoken, it is time to present the newly named tribal member with the gifts of wisdom.

Next, the tribe should decorate the celebrant with the face paint, and co-create a headdress adorned with feathers, beads, and other embellishments, making it as magnificent as possible. This headdress is the insignia of new-the found member.

Drum, rattle, and sing on this new moon night, as an important new member of the tribe has just come into being! After the festivities, the newly anointed activist should help clean up and close the circle as they now have sacred duties to the tribe.

WITCH CRAFT
Make Your Own Ceremonial Drum

Did you know that drums are the oldest musical instrument of humankind? In use since time immemorial, the beat of the drum is woven into the fabric of the past, the present, and the future. Calling a ritual to order with a drum feels deeply natural—you can feel the vibration in your very bones. Creating your own drums for rituals and meetings is a straightforward and highly enjoyable group activity.

First, make a pair of drumsticks. Make a hole in each cork stopper with a corkscrew, fill the holes with glue, and push a skewer into each hole. Wrap a few lengths of cord around the ends of the skewers so they will be comfortable in your hands during use.

Roll the can in a piece of colorful paper and use the pencil to mark the top and bottom of the can. Cut out this strip of paper and glue it around the outside of the can.

Cut the balloon at the neck and gently stretch it out. Place the balloon in the can and gently stretch the balloon over the can. This is the surface you will be using as a drum. Now wrap a length of the cord or rope around the balloon edge and glue to secure it to the paper. Let everything dry and set.

Each drum costs only pennies to create and is a wonderfully imaginative way to upcycle old cans. You can use small cans and many sizes to create a DIY drum set.

Gather Together

2 cork stoppers, available from craft stores

Corkscrew

Strong glue

2 wooden skewers

Cord or rope, at least 1ft (30cm) in length

A can (a recycled coffee container is ideal)

Colorful paper

Pencil

Scissors

Balloon

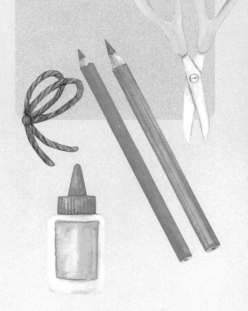

CHAPTER 8

CO-CREATING BLESSINGS

**Rituals for Groups
and Solo Spellcasters**

Goddess-Blessed Service
of the Mind and Heart

There is such a thing as magical thinking. Learning how to reframe your mindset to one of abundance for all is key to activism for change.

An abundance mindset is the opposite of a deprivation mindset. So many of us were not raised with an attitude of plenty. With many working long hours and doing all they can to make ends meet, it is not always easy to envision effortless flowing of plenitude.

When you change the way you think and talk, it shifts everything. The discipline of editing out certain words and thought patterns can influence what is available to you, your family, and your collective. It is important to realize that this is not selfishness—you and your fellow activists are pooling your energy and efforts to help feed children, provide shelter for the homeless, and to educate and build opportunities for those who need a helping hand. That is goddess-blessed work of the heart and of the highest level of service to humanity.

Intention-Setting for a Better World

Daily Morning Intention

Every morning, before I even open my eyes, I set a daily intention. I visualize how my day is going to be and I then state aloud my intention for it to turn out well. This practice takes only a few moments, but it sets a positive tone so I can begin each day calm, grounded, and centered.

Below is an example of a recent intention I made. And I intend it to work extremely well for you! Your ritual is just for you, and your visualizations and intentions should work with your daily routine.

- As We Receive More, So Shall We Give More

- May Everyone Have All They Need

- Live Long and Prosper

Here's my intention: "I intend today's activist writing to flow easily and result in messages that will inspire people, fill their hearts and minds with positive energy, and help them to defend our planet."

Now set your own intention! Your intention should be:

- Clear and simple

- Positive

- Exclude any limiting beliefs

When you have decided what you want, state your intention—vocalize it or write it down.

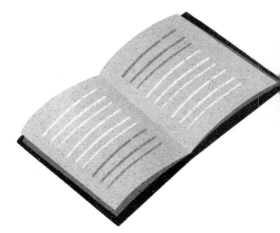

Edit These Phrases Out of Your Life

I was fortunate indeed to work with a spiritual group who held classes and meetings designed to help you embrace an abundance mentality. It does not happen overnight, and I keep this list of words handy to review whenever I catch myself sinking into a deprivation outlook. Here is a useful list of phrases to edit out of your thoughts and vocabulary:

Why is everything always so difficult for me?

Some things never change.

There's no way this is going to work out.

It's too late.

So-and-so is incapable of changing; they're a lost cause.

It doesn't look very promising.

I'm getting sick and tired of all this.

What a struggle this is.

The weather is getting worse.

There's nothing we can do about it.

New Moon Cooperative

COLLECTIVE INTENTION-SETTING RITE

It is important to maintain harmony within your group by reaffirming your collective intentions. When your statements are written down and posted where they can be seen, it reinforces the passion and purpose of the group. These gatherings are a wonderful way to concretize your mission, not only for your members, but also for the world—the statements can be used as protest march posters or displayed in offices, gathering places, and the front windows of homes.

On the day of a new moon, set out the paper and markers on the table and invite the collective to gather. The leader of the ritual should talk about intention-setting and give an example of an intention that relates to the work of the collective. For example, a recent intention of mine was: "I intend for racism to end, for fear to give way to acceptance and the understanding that we are all members of the human race. No more hate; only love."

Invite everyone to select paper and pens and call for quiet time while the group composes their intentions. As each person finishes, they can sit down in respectful silence as others work. Once every attendee is seated, take turns around the circle to stand up, show, and state each activist intention. After all have spoken, the group should say together, "So mote it be."

Display the intention statements in your regular meeting place until the next meeting or the next full moon. When folks take back their written statements, encourage them to post them where they can see them every day. This will strengthen the power of the intention.

Gather Together

A large table, to use as an altar and workspace

Large sheets of blank paper

Colorful markers, at least four for each attendee

Chairs, arranged in a circle

People Are Resources, Too

Vanquishing Psychic Vampires

Time is enormously valuable. How should you spend it? This is an area of utmost importance and requires careful consideration—if something isn't helping you in life, or advancing the causes of your collective or coven, maybe it is not worth your time.

It is an unfortunate truth that some people are psychic vampires— those who make unfair demands on your time and energy—and it is tremendously important to guard yourself against them. How to recognize the signs of a vampire? Perhaps there is someone you know who, no matter how much you try to keep the conversation positive, will heap on the woe by the bucketload. After you've talked with this person even for a few moments, you feel the positive energy draining out of your body. You've just encountered a psychic vampire!

Perhaps psychic vampires are not aware of their incessant chi draining but when you fall victim to their negative energy, you are giving away your power. In the last few years, as I age and sage, I have developed a growing awareness that time is the most precious resource and must be protected.

How to Shield Your Personal Energy as an Activist

The best defense is a strong, positive attitude and sense of self. You would not leave your house on a cold, windy day without a coat, right? Well, don't leave your house without a psychic shield—you'll thank yourself later.

Visualize a secure defense against unwarranted psychic intruders. Some folks visualize garage doors, others a big, protective blanket, and I have even heard of some who imagine being enclosed in a shell like an egg. My aura shield is a visualization of a favorite hooded robe. The more you practice your meditation and creative visualization, the greater your skill will grow.

Common Ground

RIGHT ALIGNMENT RITE

A collective dedicated to making this world a better place is likely to be a passionate group of people. This is perfect for getting great things accomplished, but it can be tricky—not everyone is going to agree on everything all the time.

It is important to remain aligned as a group and tend your mission regularly with discussion and rites that bring everyone back together. The new moon is a perfect time to infuse your collective with shared purpose and mutual support.

WITCH CRAFT
Opening the Doors to Change

Gather Together

A bundle of lavender

A bundle of rosemary

A handful of pine branches

5 long-stemmed white roses

5 cinnamon sticks

5 vanilla beans (pods)

Several lengths of raffia

Yellow and green ribbons

If your group has a dedicated meeting space, or if one of your homes is the unofficial office, you can set the stage for good meetings and good works with an easy-to-make wreath that will open the door to change every single time the door is used.

Gather all the elements together in an attractive bundle, then wrap with the raffia, and tie securely. Wrap the ribbons over the raffia and arrange in a bow or let them cascade down. Affix the door hanging you have created to the front door as you would any front door wreath. Every visitor will bring more blessings and positive change!

On the day of a new moon, place chairs around a small altar table at your home or meeting space. Place the candle, sweetgrass or smudging sage, fireproof dish, and the pen and paper on the table. When the group is gathered, ask everyone to consider what they want to say about your shared mission and what they want to bring to the group.

Light the candle and the bundle of sweetgrass or smudging sage with the matches. If there are scent sensitivities, there is no need to light the herbs—you can simply pass the unlit herbs around for their grounding properties and light only the candle. Speak the following aloud:

Our common ground brings us together

Though we come from every walk of life.

We all bring something unique to the table

Though we have very different ideas.

Our purpose binds us strongly together.

We are so aligned, bound by our mutual purpose.

With patience and mutual respect, we stand together.

And so it is.

Invite all the attendees to take a few minutes to compose their personal mission statement for the collective using the paper and pens provided. This should be a quiet time for contemplation. If it does not affect any attendees' allergies or health in any way, sage the room with the smudging stick while everyone writes their statement.

Everyone should read their statement aloud. Once everyone has finished, repeat the chant and place the statements on the altar. Extinguish the smudging stick and the candle and keep it at the ready for the next Right Alignment Rite.

Gather Together

A stool or small table, to use as a temporary altar

Chairs (enough for everybody)

A large, white soy candle in a glass votive

A bundle of sweetgrass or smudging sage, to make a smudging stick

A fireproof dish

Pen and paper for each participant

Matches

Ancient Wisdom for Modern Times: Protective Talismans

Protection Magic for Your Change Warriors

A talisman is an object that also provides protection and has magical properties. Ancient peoples, including the Mesopotamians, Assyrians, Babylonians, and Egyptians, loved animal talismans for the qualities associated with different animals for courage—bulls for virility, cats for stealth, and so on. A talisman can be any article or symbol that you believe has magical properties. As we have discussed, many gems and crystals naturally have very special innate powers. With talismanic magic, the special powers have to be either present through nature or summoned in the context of a ritual in which the magic is instilled. Even though people often confuse amulets with talismans, they differ in this significant way: amulets passively protect the wearer from harm and evil or negativity, while talismans are active in their transformative powers. For example, the supernatural sword Excalibur, a talisman imbued with supremacy by the Lady of the Lake, gave King Arthur magical powers. Another way to look at it is that talismans are created for a specific task, while amulets have broader uses. So an amulet can be worn all the time for general protection, whereas a talisman is for a specific use and a narrower aim. The varieties of talismans are many: for love, wealth, gambling, the gift of a silver tongue, a good memory, or the prevention of death. Whatever you can think of, there is probably a talisman for that exact purpose!

Enchanted Amulets

It is courageous to protest and speak out loudly and proudly about your causes but, as we know, not everyone you encounter will agree—and some you meet on your path might really disagree. Wearing a protective amulet is a marvelous reminder to be street smart and keep the peace.

Amulets are very easy to make, and as long as your friend is aware of the special qualities and power of the stone, make nice gifts that will truly benefit. Select a stone that is endowed with the energy you desire (see box below for a list of stones and the specific kinds of safeguard they offer). Hold the stone in the palm of your hand until it is warm from your touch. Then visualize the gift the stone is offering. Wear your amulet as a pendant or tuck it in your pocket or purse for a "guardian to go."

Power Gems for Every Day of the Week

Amber: One of the oldest of talismans, containing great power for general safety.

Amethyst: Helps with sobriety by preventing inebriation.

Aquamarine: A guard against malevolent spirits, this stone is also useful if you want to attract wisdom or have a fear of water and drowning.

Bloodstone: Lucky and good to wear when traveling.

Carnelian: This stone is to devils what garlic is to a vampire—it keeps 'em away.

Chrysolite: Drives away evil spirits and aids peaceful sleep, especially if set in gold.

Diamond: In the form of a necklace, diamonds bring good fortune and should always touch the skin. This dazzling stone works best when it is received as a gift; it lends force and valor.

Emerald: Cancel the power of any magician!

Jade: Offers protection to children and guards their health. Jade also creates prosperity power.

Jasper: Reputed to be a defense against the venom of poisonous insects and snakes.

Jet: Expels negativity, especially when set in silver.

Moonstone: A boon to travelers and also brings fortune and fame.

Holy Grails

Magic Cup Ritual

A chalice is a goblet dedicated specifically for use on your altar. Holding both liquid and the reservoirs of our emotional body, it is elementally connected to Water. While cauldrons are the magical tool that signify female energy (see page 94), a chalice is the symbol for male energy. A chalice is also a grail—King Arthur's legend recounts how the holy grail brought the decaying kingdom at Camelot back to life, restoring Arthur and his people and giving rise to the rebirth of England itself.

On your altar, your chalice can hold water, mead, wine, juice, or anything you deem appropriate as an offering to share with the deities. They are also remarkably useful for bonding and celebration in group rituals—after conducting the business of your group it is inspiring to toast to a job well done by drinking from chalices and speaking a sacred toast.

For this fun magic cup ritual, gather enough wine goblets and beer mugs for everyone in your cooperative. All of them being different from each other will add to the charm of the ritual. Celebrate with a herbal recipe (see pages 74–77) or bring a sparkling cider, wine, or beer to share. The ritual leader should lay out the chalices, goblets, and mugs on a small table, gather everyone into a circle around the table, and speak this blessing aloud:

Here, on this blessed day,

We acknowledge our hard work.

We honor our good deeds.

Here, on this blessed day,

We toast a job well done

By one and all!

Bright blessings unfold

For one and all!

So mote it be!

The ritual leader should pour some of the libation into a chalice, serving one person at a time. Once everyone has a full cup, each person can toast using their own inspired language. If this ritual takes on the atmosphere of a party, all the better. Blessed be!

Secrets to Finding Fairy Folk

There are benevolent beings all around us. Stay relaxed and alert in your herb garden, nearby park, or a favorite grove of trees, because fairies could be close. Some may well be right behind the tall, flowering shrub on your front path! Other tips to increase the possibility of an encounter with the enchanted fairy realm include:

- Remember your own sense of playfulness

- Spend time in nature, the element of the fae

- Practice mindfulness through meditation and relaxation

- Grow the flowers and herbs that attract them

- Make offerings to the fairies, such as a nature altar

- Sing!

Ask Good Fairies to Help Your Cause

Fairy folk are often overjoyed to be a part of your life and can assist you in so many ways.

The wee ones are playful and will appear in your peripheral vision, so you might catch a glimmer or a sudden sparkle akin to fireflies. If you are suddenly captivated by an enticing floral aroma, this is very likely to be a visitor as they can manifest in a lovely scent, as well. A mysterious little chime or tinkling bell is also a fairy sign. When you have a sense that the fairies near your home are comfortable being in your presence by giving you two of these signs, you can ask them for aid.

Your request can be direct but gentle, respectful, and appreciative. An example might be: "Dearest Fairies, we ask you to ensure our march will be completely peaceful this Friday. We ask to be well received in our purpose and respected. We will strive to do the same. Thank you, gentle ones."

As thanks for their help, leave an offering such as a teaspoon of honey at the base of a flower. Good fairy energy is very sweet and gentle. Return it in kind.

How One Inspired Act Can Change the World

Get acquainted with simple human kindness and easy acts of goodness every day. I am blessed to have been part of the team that brought Random Acts of Kindness to the world (see Resources, page 141), an organization dedicated to incorporating kindness into your life by adopting a kindly mindset, and it was a highlight of my career.

When at the grocery store, return the shopping cart or help the elderly man struggling with his bags. Open doors for people. Say "hello" with a smile. Every day, and in every way, choose to take the high road in your travels. The view is much more beautiful from up top!

Instant Kindness: Look Up!

Put down your smartphone and make eye contact, person to person. Nowadays, I consider that a major act of kindness, and courtesy as well.

DIY Optimism

Try this easy way to craft some kindness. Make a sign that reads, "Take what you need" with tear-off tabs on the bottom that say, "love," "courage," "optimism," and so on. Hang up the sign in places you regularly pass by. Keep refills at the ready!

Optimism

Courage

Love

Resources

Eco Sustainable Solutions
www.thisiseco.co.uk/news/what-is-xeriscaping/

Information about organic recycling, including garden solutions such as xeriscaping.

Food Not Bombs
www.foodnotbombs.net

An all-volunteer movement that redistributes discarded vegan and vegetarian food to the hungry.

Freecycle
www.freecycle.org

A global, non-profit movement for people to give, receive and exchange items for free in their own towns.

Freegan
www.freegan.info

Strategies for everyday living based on sharing resources, reducing consumption, and recyling waste.

Glide
www.glide.org

A San Francisco-based center for social justice with an extensive Volunteer Resource Program.

Little Free Library
www.littlefreelibrary.org

An information-sharing resource based on the concept of "take a book, leave a book," little free libraries have inspired food-sharing resources such as little free pantries.

Random Acts of Kindness Foundation
www.randomactsofkindness.org

Kindness resources to help you bring more kindness into the world.

WM
www.wm.com/us/en/inside-wm/
sustainable-technology/organics-recycling

Information about organic recycling and composting, including residential waste and recycling pick-up.

Continue Your Journey:

Gardner, Gerald, *The Meaning of Witchcraft* (Aquarian, 1959)

Greenleaf, Cerridwen, *The Book of Witchy Wellbeing* (Cico Books, 2021)

Read, Donna, *The Burning Times* (documentary, 1990)

Index

abundance
  abundance mindset 129, 131
  see also money magic
altars
  abundance altar 98–99
  altar plants 18–19
  candles 10–11
  for change 9–11
  compass points 60
  crystals 16–17
  four-elements altar 14–15
  gods and goddesses 20–23
amulets 136, 137

bamboo 34
basil 18–19, 76, 105
besom blessings 51–52
borage 37
Brazilian candomblé ritual 39
butterfly bush 37

candles 10–11, 88
  battery-operated 27
  candle blessing spells 11, 47
  candle vigils 47–48
  sigils 83
  soy wax 10–11
cauldrons 94, 109, 138
  cauldron money magic 62
chamomile 77, 107
change pot 62
charms
  drought prevention charm 31
  money bag charm 110–111
cinnamon 19, 105
climate change 26, 57, 108
color energies 46
community gardens 58
consciousness-raising ritual
  80–81
covens 6, 51, 71, 116
cow parsnip 37
crystals 16–17, 88
  power gems 84–85, 137

dahlias 37
daisies 37
dandelions 38
The Diggers 63
door wreath 134
drought 30, 57
  drought prevention charm 31
drum, ceremonial 127
dumpster diving 63

echinacea 37
encouragement, offering 55, 92
equinox equality ritual 60–61
essential oils 12–13, 47

fairy folk 37, 107, 139
feminist activism 70–95
Feng Shui 102
flags
  intention flags 28
  scattering blessings 52
  Tibetan prayer flags 52
floor cleansing 100–101
Flora incantation 68–69
food and food activism 56–69
  chocolate cake 113
  community garden produce 59
  dumpster diving 63
  fundraising foods 112–113
  grain spell 65
  healthy harvest 65
  Little Free Pantry 58
  moon cakes 67
  resource justice 64
  urban foraging 63
  volunteering 57
Food Not Bombs 63
four elements 14–15
Freecycle 63
Freegans 63
fundraising activism 109–113

gardens
  community garden 58

guerrilla gardening 34–35, 36
  keeping green 34
  rain barrel 30, 34
  xeriscaping 34
goldenrod 38
gourd rattle 123
grain spell 65
grass mulch 34
gun violence 48

hawthorn 75, 107
hedge witches 51, 75
hot foot protection powder 82
hunger 57
  food *see* food

incense 15, 23
  incense ceremony 91
ink, magic 73

Johnny Appleseed 35

Kali 22

lavender 18, 38
leaf composting 34
Little Free Library 58
Little Free Pantry 58

magic cup ritual 138
magical thinking 129
mantras 16
marigolds 38, 107
mask-making 92–93
migrants and refugees
  29, 57, 71, 108
milkweed 38
mimosa 76
money magic 97–113
  fundraising activism 109–113
  health and wealth chai 106
  herbal money brew 104
  herbs and spices 105
  lucky 13 fund-raising ritual 109

money bag charm 110–111
money tree 103
money-drawing altar
  blessing 99
sending abundance from
  afar 108
wealth corner 102
Moon 124–125
  Full Moon teachings 49
  New Moon invocation of
    Hecate 50
moon cakes 67
muses 86, 87

Naiads 33
nasturtiums 35
Native Americans 49, 65, 66, 120

oat milk 76
Orishas 39–41, 118–119
  making an offering to 41

passionflower 77
peace activism 42–55
Peace Pilgrim 53
peace-making ritual 54
persecution of witches 95, 116
pine 19
planetary activism 24–41
plants
  altar plants 18–19
  green magic seed spell 34
  money magic 105, 107
  money tree 103
  pollinators 37–38
  seed bombs 36
prayers, intentions and
    meditations
  for an end to gun violence 48
  daily intention 130
  for inner and world peace 53
  intention flags 28
  intention-setting rites
    26–27, 132

moving meditation 53
  for the planet 26–27
  for resource justice 64
  sending abundance from
    afar 108
  to support people at a
    distance 89
  touchstone meditation 16
  water deity invocation 32
protest marches 44, 72
  post-protest ritual 78–79
  protest signs 45–46, 72
psychic shield 133
psychic vampires 133

rain barrel, making a 30, 34
Random Acts of Kindness 140
rituals
  before a protest march 44
  bound by purpose ritual 29
  Brazilian candomblé ritual 39
  consciousness-raising
    ritual 80–81
  equinox equality ritual 60–61
  Flora incantation 68–69
  intention-setting rituals
    26–27, 132
  invoking ancestor guides
    120–121
  lucky 13 fund-raising ritual 109
  magic cord ritual 29
  magic cup ritual 138
  mask-making 92–93
  money-drawing altar
    blessing 99
  peace-making ritual 54
  planetary ritual 26–27
  post-protest ritual 78–79
  right alignment ritual 134–135
  soul tribe ritual 83
  spider wisdom ritual 66
rosemary 19

Salem Witch Trials 95

Santería 118
scrying 94
shrines 88
sigils 83
skullcap 76
smudging 18, 122
snapdragons 38
social justice activism 114–127
solidarity, creating 88
soul tribe 83, 88, 90
spells
  attraction magic 90
  besom blessings 51–52
  candle blessing spells 11, 47
  grain spell 65
  green magic seed spell 34
  New Moon invocation
    of Hecate 50
  prosperity for all spell 62
  for protection 82
  sacred smoke spell 122
spider wisdom ritual 66
sunflowers 38, 107

talismans 136
tea
  health and wealth chai 106
  herbal teas 74, 75–77, 104, 105
  money brew 104
  tea ceremony 74
Thich Nhat Hanh 53
Tibetan mythology 52
Tibetan prayer flags 52

urban foraging 63

water deities 32, 33
Wicca 115, 116–117
wildfires 39, 43

xeriscaping 34

yarrow 75
Yoruban spirituality 39, 118

Acknowledgments

This book was truly a collaboration with the marvelous Kristine Pidkameny and a deep alignment of intention. My great hope is that this book brings good to the world and much-needed positive change. I know Kristine and Team CICO feel exactly the same. I am lucky to be published by folks who care so much about crafting beautiful books and I feel especially grateful about this wonderfully positive experience. Big thanks to editor Kristy Richardson who improved the book immensely and to the illustrator, Barbara Tamilin, and designers, Sally Powell and Emily Breen, who turned my words and ideas into art. Much thankfulness to the Publishing Manager Penny Craig and her extraordinary team at CICO Books.

Picture Credits

All illustrations by Barbara Tamilin except the following:

@Adobe Stock/ **Olgahalizeva** 20; **s_shimko** page 22 (top); **zzorik** 30. 34; **zlata_titmouse** 33 (top); **Kindlena** 33 (bottom); **mlanaa** 44 (top and bottom), 78 (top and bottom), 79 (center and bottom), 89 (bottom), 108 (right), 118, 119 (bottom); **Romispring** 44 (center), 54 (top), 55 (top and bottom), 78 (center), 79 (top), 131, 140; **Evgeniia** 50 (top and bottom); **Volodymyr** 66 (left); **NATALIIA TOSUN** 66 (right); **Claire** 67; **AYSIA** 80 (bottom) and 81 (bottom); **annakonchits** 75 (center); **ElenaMedvedeva** 76 (top), 77 (top); **depiano** 76 (bottom); **Toshka** 77 (center); **Tatiana Ka** 82 (right); **Chica** 86 (top), 87; **Svetlana** 86 (bottom), 93, 123 (bottom), 127 (bottom), 133 (top); **atichat** 88 (right); **Marina Lahereva** 92 (bottom); **madamsaffa** 92 (top); 夏妃 吉野 101 (right), 105 (center), 106, 108; **violet** 113 (bottom); **ogurechka** 113 (center); **cosmicanna** 113 (top); **anitapol** 116 (bottom); **Anna Terleeva** 119 (top); **jill** 123 (top); **Julija** 126; **Elizaveta** 127 (top). **Victoria Fomina:** ages 28, 30 (bottom), 32 (background), 64, 72, 124–125 (background), 125 (bottom), 130 (top right), 139 (bottom) **Emma Garner:** pages 5, 14, 15 (top), 20 (top), 26 (top right), 31, 32 (top), 40, 45 (bottom), 49, 51 (bottom left), 52, 58, 60, 61 (top), 62 (centre and bottom), 69, 73 (left and top), 74 (bottom), 77 (bottom), 83 (left), 85 (bottom), 90, 91, 100 (bottom left), 101 (top), 102 (bottom), 103 (top right and bottom), 107, 110 (top), 116 (bottom), 117 (bottom right), 120–121, 122 (bottom), 124, 125 (top), 132, 134 (top), 136 (left and top right), 136 (centre right), **Camila Gray:** pages 39 (background), 91 **Roy Palmer** (photographer): pages 17, 85 (top).